Pacific

Ocean

TA ISABEL
...AND

FLORIDA
ISLAND

MALAITA
ISLAND

Tulagi
SAVO I.
CAPE
ESPERANCE   *Sealark Channel*
KOLI   *Lengo Channel*
PT.
Kokumbona   *Tassafaronga*

ULAWA IS.

GUADALCANAL
ISLAND

SAN CRISTOBAL
ISLAND

HARRY GARDNER -'45

ACTION TONIGHT

by James D. Horan

OUT IN THE BOONDOCKS (*with Gerold Frank*)

ACTION TONIGHT

DEATH BY NIGHT

Action Tonight

THE STORY OF THE DESTROYER

O'Bannon IN THE PACIFIC

BY JAMES D. HORAN

WITH 20 OFFICIAL U. S. NAVY PHOTOGRAPHS

G. P. PUTNAM'S SONS, NEW YORK

IMPORTANT

Government wartime restrictions on mate-
rials have made it essential that the
amount of paper used in each book be re-
duced to a minimum. This volume is
printed on lighter paper than would have
been used before material limitations became necessary, and the number of words
on each page has been substantially increased. The smaller bulk in no way indi-
cates that the text has been shortened.

Designed by Robert Josephy

To the valiant officers and men
of the United States destroyers
and in particular to that gallant
ship, the U.S.S. *O'Bannon*.

ACKNOWLEDGMENT

Many naval officers have been helpful in the preparation and technical criticism of this book and it is impossible to name them all. But the author wishes to express his especial gratitude to the office of Commander Walter Karig's Magazine and Book Section of the U. S. Navy Public Relations Office and to Commander H. A. MacDonald, USNR, of the Motion Picture Section, United States Navy.

Many officers and men who saw action aboard the *O'Bannon* have been of great help to the author in telling this story; particularly Commander Donald J. MacDonald, Lt. Comdr. Robert C. Manchester, Lt. D. B. Eardley, Lt. J. J. Noonan, Lt. I. R. Fahrbach, Chief Radioman E. H. Padgett, Chief Watertender M. M. Zimmerman, Louis F. Cianca, Cox 3/c, T. T. Miller, GM 3/c, R. H. Fleming, WT 2/c, Chief Controlman James O. Bess. Also Margaret Erbe and Sadye Gabbe for stenographic assistance; and Gertrude, Jen, and Wally who suffered through it all.

FOREWORD

The history of the Pacific war can never be written without telling the story of the U.S.S. *O'Bannon*.

Time after time the *O'Bannon* and her gallant little sisters were called upon to turn back the enemy. They never disappointed me.

Out-numbered, out-gunned, during the dark days of '42 and '43 they stood toe-to-toe with the best the Japanese Fleet could offer—and never failed to send them scurrying home with their tails between their legs.

No odds were ever too great for them to face. They fought battleships and heavy cruisers; escorted vitally needed supply ships for marines on Guadalcanal; bombarded Japanese positions; aided in dangerous rescue operations; and derailed the Tokio Express so often that the Japanese admirals ran out of excuses.

No medals, however high, can reward the gallant men of the tin-can fleet for their brave deeds.

In her darkest hour their country called. They answered with flaming guns and high courage.

This is their story.

WILLIAM F. HALSEY
Admiral, U.S. Navy

CONTENTS

Foreword by Admiral William F. Halsey   vii

1   The U.S.S. *O'Bannon*, Queen of the Tin-Can Fleet   1

2   War Touches the *O'Bannon*   17

3   The Battle of Guadalcanal   25

4   Munda Bombardment   47

5   Bombardment of Vila-Stanmore   59

6   Double Bombardment of Munda and Vila-Stanmore   66

7   Battle of the Submarine   72

8   Battle of Kolombangara   89

9   Kula Gulf   99

10   Surface Action off Kolombangara Island   113

11   Rescue of the *Helena* Survivors   122

12   Auckland—Pappy Gets His Food Supply   132

13   Barge Hunting   137

14   Vella Lavella   142

15   Home   157

Presidential Unit Citation   161

Officers and Men of the *O'Bannon*   162

Sixteen pages of Photographic Illustrations Follow Page   86

ACTION TONIGHT

1 THE U.S.S. O'BANNON,
Queen of the Tin-Can Fleet

THE CAB HAD reached the top of the hill just past Bath's Congregational Church when Chief Gunner's Mate LeRoy Spracklin got his first glimpse of the ship. After a quick glance he leaned over to the driver,

"You better stop this gig, mate, I think you're on the wrong bearing."

The cab jerked to a stop, tires skidding on the muddy road. A pair of light blue eyes, set deep in a face weather-beaten until it resembled well-used teak, looked back at him.

"You wanted that new destroyer, the *O'Bannon*, didn't you, son?"

Spracklin nodded. "But that's no destroyer you're taking me to, Pop, that's a light cruiser. Hell, cans are smaller and kinda squat."

The cab driver scowled. "When we build ships up here, son, we don't make them 'kinda squat.'" He repeated the phrase with a touch of irritation in his voice. "People here have been building ships since before the Revolution and they've had a lot of practice."

He pointed to the Bath Iron Works sprawled along the Kennebec River at the foot of the hill.

"Down there's the ship you want. Hell, everybody knows the *O'Bannon* in this town. There hasn't been as much talk about a ship around these parts since they built the ninety-day gunboats

Katahdin and *Iosco* my grandpappy worked on during the Civil War."

To see better, Spracklin rolled down the window of the cab, but he still wasn't satisfied. He opened the door and stood on the running board. Now he could see clear across the Kennebec River, sparkling in the spring sunshine.

At the foot of the hill was the tidy little city of Bath, sloping upward from the broad river. Above the city, the hills closed, touched here and there by the first green signs of spring. Beyond the city's limits were fertile squares of red and green farmlands disappearing in a wide expanse of hazy flats and rolling hills. This was Bath, Maine, birthplace of America's shipbuilding. But Spracklin's eyes were glued to a ship that lay alongside one of the docks in the yard. She was long, slim, and beautiful. From the high sharp bow to the neatly rounded fantail, she was compact, powerful. She was such a far cry from any other destroyer he had ever seen that Spracklin whistled in admiration.

"Beauty isn't she?" the cab driver said. But the chief gunner's mate didn't answer. His glance was moving over the ship, touching almost affectionately the sleek gray hull; the bridge structure breaking away sharply, like a small steel cliff, to the torpedo deck with its spread of torpedo tubes—nearly as long as the ship was wide—mounted midships. Scattered about the destroyer, on the main deck, weather deck, flying bridge, and fantail, he noted the pencil points of 20-mm. guns. Just aft of smokestack Number Two, and on the fantail, were depth charges, stacked together in their iron racks.

But again and again, like steel drawn to a magnet, Spracklin's eyes came back to the *O'Bannon's* five 5-inch gun mounts. Five 5-inchers!

"Somebody is going to get hurt when that baby gets mad," he said half aloud.

Spracklin looked the ship over again and made a quick estimate. "About 350 feet," he said. "Smaller than a keel I saw laid down in Portsmouth last week but that barge didn't have the lines of this beauty."

"She's 376 feet long," the cab driver volunteered. Spracklin turned around.

"How do you know, Pop?"

The old man grinned. "Ever since they put her keel down the boys in the Bath Iron Works have been acting like they're expecting a baby. That's all you hear in town. O' course we all agree with them. Think she's a great ship. Probably the best this town has put out in years. She's a ship to be proud of, son."

Spracklin had heard enough. He was seized with a sudden eagerness to feel the *O'Bannon's* steel plates under his feet. He wanted to get a look inside those gun mounts. He wanted to see those breeches. He hoped they had watched the yard workmen putting them into place. . . .

"Come on, Pop," he growled, "let's get going. There's a war on."

At the same moment that Spracklin stepped back into his cab, deep in the *O'Bannon's* forward fireroom Chief Watertender Mack Zimmerman was asking Chief Watertender Judson Unroe,

"What do you think she'll do?"

Unroe grunted. He was a powerfully built man, with bushy thick black eyebrows and hands that looked like red boxing gloves.

"Pfeifer said she could do about thirty-four knots with all boilers if she had to."

He patted a stainless-steel boiler.

"Remember the firerooms in those four-pipers, Zip?"

Zimmerman grinned. Many an hour he had toiled in the dim steamy holes, nursing worn-out fireboxes, cursing useless equipment, and praying for a transfer.

Unroe gave a tug at his dungarees. No matter how often he tugged they always seemed to slip below his stomach. He grunted as he remembered the nights the old destroyers rolled and the bunk chains dug into your sides leaving ugly black-and-blue bruises. He thought of the chief's quarters forward on the *O'Bannon*. "Dammit," he said, "this war certainly has made changes for the chiefs."

3

He looked around the fireroom.

"Not only for men but for ships," he observed. "What a beauty this *O'Bannon* is . . . 2,100 tons, Christ, she's built like a light cruiser . . . five 5-inchers . . . Pappy Rowland for a cook . . . God, what more could we want?"

He grinned at Zimmerman.

"This baby is the queen of the whole damn tin-can fleet, Zip," he said. The other chief nodded.

"You're not kidding," he said.

On deck, the *O'Bannon*'s commissary chief, Melvin "Pappy" Rowland, stepped out of the forward hatch leading from the CPO's quarters and walked across the forecastle to lean on the lifeline, a railing formed of three steel cables, which fenced in the destroyer from bow to fantail.

He dug deep in his dungarees and took out a small tin box of Copenhagen snuff. He took a generous pinch, rolled it around his mouth until it found its familiar resting place between his cheek and lower jaw, then leaned over the water and spit to leeward. The snuff made a small mound like a walnut in his cheek —and it wasn't unusual for new shipmates to stop "Pappy" on deck and solicitously inquire if he had a toothache. In fact, on all the cans Pappy had served during his twenty years in the Navy, there was always some chief who had heard of his snuff-chewing habit and would pass the word along until Pappy couldn't walk ten paces without crew members stopping him to say:

"That's a bad tooth you've got there, Pappy, why don't you have it yanked?" Rowland would snort and threaten to poison all coffeepots, but it was always good for a chuckle with the CPO's sitting over a cup of steaming black coffee after a late watch.

Pappy looked down the weather deck, stretching like a narrow iron corridor from the forecastle to aft of the spud locker at the base of Number Two stack. Just midships, at the gangway, he could see Lieutenant Lanson Ditto, Jr., who had the deck, talking to someone in a passageway. Draped around his middle was a heavy holster and gun which hung off his side, giving him a peculiar, lopsided look. As he watched, a young sea-

man walked aboard and started for the passageway. Rowland heard Lieutenant Ditto call the boy back. The officer said something sharply and motioned to the ensign flying on the stern. The boy moved back to the gangway, saluted, and formally reported to Ditto. Pappy shook his head in disgust. He leaned over the side, spit again, and stood looking across the yard.

"Thinking, Rowland?" a soft voice inquired.

The chief turned to look into the quiet brown eyes of the executive officer of the *O'Bannon*, Lieutenant-Commander Donald J. MacDonald. The officer was smoking a pipe, and the blue smoke curled about his square chin and firm lips.

The chief cleared his throat.

"I was thinking, Mr. MacDonald," he said slowly, "of how green our crew is." He paused, but as he suddenly remembered how a boy he met only that morning had asked, "Which is the front of the boat, Chief?" he groaned and said, "God, sir, they certainly are green."

MacDonald nodded. He tapped his pipe against the lifeline, and both men watched the sparks and ashes fly across the water.

"Well, Rowland," he said, "they are green. They are probably greener than any crew a press gang ever sent to Nelson. But I wouldn't do too much worrying about them. We'll take them out to sea and make seamen out of them, you wait and see if we don't. There's good material there, Rowland. It's up to all of us to develop it."

He nodded and walked down the weather deck. Every step he took was firm, sure.

During his twenty years of naval service, Pappy Rowland had served in many stations, from the States to the Far East. To him officers had come to mean something quite impersonal; they were men who wore gold braid and had authority. Some whom he'd met had been smart, some incompetent, some just plain stupid. But as he watched his executive officer walk along the deck, he was thoughtful.

"Dammit," he told himself, "I guess he's right. Hell, we got the best damn ship in the fleet, and there's no reason we can't have the best crew. Just wait until the chiefs get going."

He pushed his hat at a rakish angle and his eyes gleamed behind his steel-rimmed glasses. He moved his lips, so that the mound of snuff rolled to the other cheek. He walked over to the hatch and started down to his galley.

As Pappy Rowland passed the CPO's quarters, Chief Gunner's Mate Spracklin, who had come aboard a few hours before, was sipping at a thick china cup of steaming coffee.

He was listening to Chief Radioman E. H. Padgett, a tall well-built man who spoke slowly with the faint touch of a drawl, describe his radio gang. As he listened, Spracklin leaned back in his chair and blew large smoke rings overhead. They spread out, recoiled down the gray walls, and seeped out the hatchway.

". . . And when I walked into the radio shack," Padgett was saying, "this kid has a pencil copy of the Morse code propped up in front of him, banging away." He stopped and looked about the table almost unbelievingly.

"He's one of my radiomen second class and he doesn't know the Morse code."

Chief Yeoman Irvin Fahrbach, drumming on the table with a pencil, shook his head with a sigh.

"It's a fact and there's no denying it."

Across from Fahrbach, Chief Boatswain McGrath said: "I had to get them out of their sacks a few days ago, and do you know what I had to do?"

The boatswain leaned across the table and began mimicking in a high voice: "Get up boys . . . come on now and get up . . . come on kids . . ." He scowled and roared, pounding the table until Chief Fahrbach had to make a wild grab to save a coffee cup from spilling. "Then I got disgusted and yelled get up goddammit! Hit the deck . . ." He paused and said mildly,

"That got them up."

Spracklin choked on a smoke ring. Padgett laughed adroitly. Chief Torpedoman Ulrich Braun, his chest bursting through a tight blue shirt, was slapping his leg. Chief Fire Controlman James Bess—who faintly reminded everyone he met of Gary Cooper—was chuckling. When the laughter died away, their faces were ruffled by the smiles that lingered there.

6

Up in the officer's wardroom, Officer's Steward Rivers, desperately trying to remember all the details of wardroom etiquette, was bending over the captain of the *O'Bannon*, Lieutenant-Commander Edwin Wilkinson, who was scowling deeply as he cut a slice of lamb. He was listening to his engineering officer, Lieutenant Carl Pfeifer, tell Lieutenant George Philip, Jr., the gunnery officer:

". . . And so I asked him for the serial number on the turbine. There was no answer. I asked him again. No answer. Finally he said, 'I'm sorry, sir, I don't know where the turbine is.'"

The engineering officer paused for dramatic effect, then added, "And he's a machinist's mate, second class."

Philip waved his hand.

"Hell," he said, "do you know what happened when they got aboard? One kid walked up to Ditto and asked if we had any kitchens, 'because I'm very hungry.' Ditto asked the kid if he had ever been aboard a ship before and the kid said: 'Oh, yes, sir —in the Brooklyn Navy Yard on Navy Day.'"

The wardroom echoed with laughter, but Captain Wilkinson's scowl grew deeper. He was a tall, rangy man with snapping black eyes and a small mustache. Since his days on the football field he had always been called a fighter. Once a salt-crusted chief had said of him, "Wilkinson? Hell, he'll take a can and fight the devil's own navy in hell itself if they let him."

But now Captain Wilkinson felt irritated. He had a ship that was one of the finest destroyers built. She had more fire power and horsepower by far than any destroyer the Navy had. But his crew was green, not just inexperienced, but green. Some were fresh from only two weeks of boot training, plucked by the urgency of war from every walk of American life, frightened and homesick.

Just before Lieutenant Philip finished speaking, the door to the wardroom opened to admit MacDonald. He waved greetings and moved to a chair at the Captain's right. Wilkinson waved his fork at Lieutenant Philip.

"George and Carl have been informing us of the greenness of the crew, Mac," he said. "What do you think?"

7

The executive officer began buttering a slice of bread.

"I just left Rowland on deck and he seems to be worrying too, Captain," he said, helping himself to a scoop of mashed potatoes. "But I don't think it's too bad." He looked about the table, "We have a wonderful ship here."

The officers, now serious, nodded as one man.

"The boys we have are green, sure. But I've been looking them over closely the last few days and been discussing it with Captain Wilkinson. Only last night we compared notes. We both agreed that there is good material in the men we have. We can develop that material, and the result can be a fighting crew and a ship with a record in this war that we can be proud of."

Lieutenant Philip looked up. "We're with you and Captain Wilkinson in that 100 per cent, sir," he said.

Every officer at the table murmured, "Aye to that."

Meanwhile, in the crew's quarters new arrivals, stumbling between boxes and bales of bedding, made friends with older hands who sat supervising from the upper bunk tiers, gazing at their shipmates with glances both critical and friendly. Arms in skivvy shirts gesticulated between bunk chains, and voices hummed low among bursts of laughter.

"Hey, mate, grab off that bunk. . . . Where'd you shove off from boot? . . . Bainbridge? . . . I remember when I had to run that goddamn grinder four times for spitting in ranks. . . ."

Boys in blue jackets, short white shirts, dungarees mixed with half-naked bare-footed boys; others standing with blue shirts open on hairy chests pushed against each other, reeling and swaying in a blue haze of tobacco smoke. This was the *O'Bannon's* crew. Fresh from farms, east-side tenements, sleepy southern towns, Pennsylvania coal mines, high-school and college class rooms. Some who had never shaved rubbed the fuzz on their cheeks self-consciously.

Two blond giants—"We're the Conklin brothers; this here is young Conklin, I'm old Conklin"—dumped their bedding on a pile and grinned at the good-natured tempest moving about them. Above them, a short dark-skinned boy chewing on a pencil stub reached down and held out his hand:

"My name's Popino, fireman first, just call me Pop. I'll work with one of you guys in the forward fireroom. After you stow your gear, I'll show you the works." He motioned to another bunk where a husky blond boy was polishing a pair of black shoes with a tube of shaving cream. "Meet George Gregory," he said.

The boy smiled and held up the tube. "Puts a gloss on 'em," he shouted.

Another boy, as he passed, turned and said, "I'm Fleming, if I can help you let me know."

Popino nodded after him, "Arthur Fleming, watertender, second. He jumped over the side of a ship and picked up a guy in the Atlantic. Must have been cold as a welder's backside."

The *O'Bannon's* physician, Lieutenant M. Dunham, who was passing, peered through the thick tobacco smoke. The fragrance of the tobacco mixed with the heavy smell of salt water and sweating bodies. One of the new arrivals, he noticed, was stowing away a large box of chocolates.

"Be sure and tell them where sick bay is, Popino," he said. "We have plenty of castor oil on hand."

Several boys smiled and turned to look at him through the smoke.

"How's the old man?" someone asked Popino.

"Good guy."

"How's the ship?" the same voice inquired.

There was a moment of silence. Popino stopped chewing on a stub of his pencil. He looked down at the boy who asked the question. "The best, son," he said softly, "the best god damn can in the fleet."

Next morning at daylight, the *O'Bannon* went to sea. It was April, 1942.

The destination was Boston, where she was to pick up ten more members of the crew and then head out to open sea for her shakedown cruise. A slight haze blurred the sky. As they coasted past Bath, men on deck could make out the pointed spire of the Congregational Church. They watched it until it disappeared in the morning mist. The *O'Bannon* headed southward. The sea struck her with flashing blows, and as the engines picked up speed, foam bubbled about her fantail.

It was a short run. Late afternoon, as she lay at a Boston dock, the ten new crew members trooped aboard. They had just stowed their gear when the word was passed over the ship's loudspeaker:

"New hands report to Chief Bos'n McGrath on the fo'c'sle."

For ten minutes McGrath stamped impatiently on deck. Finally he sent a seaman searching for the ten men. They were found—in the fireroom.

On deck they tried to explain to the boatswain.

"Gosh, Chief," one boy said, "we've been hunting all over the ship, going upstairs and downstairs . . ."

"Up a ladder, dammit. There's no stairs on a ship," McGrath roared.

The boy gulped.

". . . Up ladders and down ladders," he repeated weakly, but the boatswain waved him into silence.

"We usually try to place men in jobs they feel they're best suited for." He nodded to a stocky, black-haired boy.

"What's your name?"

"Louis Cianca."

"Know anything about a ship?"

The boy shook his head: "Not very much, Chief."

McGrath grinned.

"You will, son." Then he added: "Do you know of any job you want to work at on the *O'Bannon?*"

The boy nodded eagerly. He pointed to the flying bridge above the pilothouse.

"I would like to be a lookout up there, Chief," he said.

McGrath raised his eyebrows.

"Are you sure you want that?"

Cianca nodded.

The Bos'n said, "Okay, go up there and tell the man there you are to stand watch with him."

Later Cianca told his bunkmates: "When I came aboard I saw a guy up on the flying bridge with a pair of binoculars, just looking around. It looked like a swell job, plenty of fresh air and sunshine, so when the Chief asked me what job I was best suited for I remembered the guy with the binoculars, so I took that. Plenty of air and sunshine for Cianca."

That night the *O'Bannon* headed out to sea on her shakedown cruise. Two days out of Boston she ran into her first storm. That morning the wind had been fresh, and the *O'Bannon* grew frolicsome with the exuberance of a light-hearted colt. Toward late afternoon it became gusty, and she heaved, pitched, and rolled with green water sweeping over her bow and foaming down across her forecastle.

Men stood their watches with buckets at their sides. Up on the flying bridge, Cianca, soaked to the skin, clung weakly to the rail.

"Fresh air and sunshine," he moaned to himself. "I wish I was back in Brooklyn."

The storm kept up for four days, but the officers and men worked from dawn to far into the night. There was barely time to eat and change into dry clothes. Formality and dress were forgotten, but discipline clamped down over the ship with a rigidity that never relaxed.

On the fourth night the storm grew worse. It was almost impossible to walk along the weather decks. Crew members caught unexpectedly by one of the giant waves would find themselves clinging desperately to the line strung along the deck, gagging and choking on seawater, which hissed triumphantly as it disappeared over the sides.

That night, Unroe and Spracklin passed the crew's quarters. They looked in at the seasick boys not on watch, sprawled out on their bunks.

"God, Sprack, I hope we can whip this mob into some kind of a crew," Unroe grunted.

Some of the boys looked up miserably as the two chiefs

stepped in. Only a few weeks before they had been living peacefully at home—most of them not yet able to vote—with the Friday-night dance, the new suit, the all-important question of money enough for that date, the only matters of import to them.

The thought of going to sea on a warship had never entered their heads, and now here they were, retching, green-faced, homesick, pitching through a heavy sea—while all about them the ship's steel body groaned in protest.

Unroe, heavy clothes dripping, stood, legs apart, clinging to a bunk chain. He looked back at Spracklin leaning against the rolling bulkhead.

"They look half dead, Sprack." Then, not unkindly, he said to the boy nearest him, "Take it easy, kid, it will wear off in about three days when you get your sea legs, and then you'll feel swell."

The *O'Bannon* lifted her bow to the sky, then started sinking to the bottom of a huge green valley as if she would never stop, while her plates creaked with the sudden wrench.

"Three more days of this," the boy moaned.

Clinging to the bunk chain, Unroe growled: "So what? When you get off this ship you'll be a destroyer man. Know what that means? It means you'll be a real sailor—not like the guys who sail around in those floating apartment houses. When the chiefs get through with you, you'll be able to tell your grandchildren you served with the best goddamn crew on the best goddamn ship in the fleet." He gave his dungarees a tug, winked at Spracklin, and walked out.

After they left, the boy Unroe spoke to reached for a galvanized bucket and croaked: "You know I think he really means it. . . . Oh, this feeling is terrible . . ."

Despite the long hours, the men bent to their work without grumbling. Classes were organized throughout the ship. In the engine room Lieutenant Pfeifer told his CPO's: "There's no substitute for doing it themselves, so keep 'em at it."

He organized classes and had written instructions attached to each valve and dial and gauge. The chiefs showed the new men how to watch the height of the water in the gauges; how to check the temperature and pressure of the oil in the burners and regulate the flow of air from the blowers so the three formed a perfect combustion. Don't waste oil; don't make smoke; too much air makes a clear stack. Watch your stack gasses, always have a light brown haze, or the old man will be on your tail. The first time they tried it a thick, black, heavy pall of smoke shrouded the ship, and Finley on the smoke watch kept screaming, "We're smoking, dammit, we're smoking,"— while Zimmerman and Unroe dashed about shouting, "Cut in air, cut in the air."

In the radio shack, Chief Padgett and Radioman First Class George Guess, who deserted the newspaper business for the Navy, rigged up a small hand key on a cigar box and kept their crew constantly practicing the code. The first night Padgett, exhausted, asked a second-class radioman,

"Tell me one thing, why did they ever put you in radio?"

The boy grinned and said: "They kept asking me in boot if I ever had anything to do with radio, so I told them I did."

Padgett raised his eyebrows.

"You were in radio before you joined up?"

The radioman chuckled.

"Yeah, I once built a crystal set," he said.

Padgett kept his radio gang sending and receiving messages in code on the homemade telegrapher's key from 8 A.M. until late in the night.

On the first day of the shakedown cruise, a gunner's mate staggered into the radio shack carrying a handful of rags.

"What the hell are you doing here with those rags?" Padgett asked.

"One of the men told me to find the periscope and give it a good cleaning," the boy said, clinging to a desk. "And I thought maybe one of you fellows could tell me where it is."

The chief radioman grinned.

"Look around the ship very thoroughly, son, and if you find it report to me at once."

The boy started out the door, then stopped:

"As soon as I find it I'll report to you, Chief?"

"You're damn right," Padgett said. "Fifteen years ago they sent me looking around for the ship's periscope and I haven't been able to find it yet."

Despite the heavy seas, torpedo and gun drills were held daily. Braun would take his men forward and form a large circle around one of the large deadly "tin fish." While the boys stood watching wide-eyed, the chief, with the confidence of a platform lecturer, would proceed to take the torpedo apart, explaining each part in detail.

After a few days torpedomen could be found clinging to the heavy steel projectiles on the rolling torpedo deck, hands plunged deep in the belly of the torpedo like a physician performing a delicate and intricate operation.

Lieutenant Philip, the gunnery officer, called his crews to the guns and put his boys, their faces green with seasickness, through brisk drilling in loading and firing. Aft, boys, with tin buckets conveniently near, stood by depth charges going through the motions of sending their "ash cans" over the side to blast an imaginary U-boat.

Target practice followed. The days preceding it Lieutenant Philip and Chief Spracklin kept the men working from dawn to sunset. Ranging, loading, simulated firing; ranging, loading, simulated firing; hour after hour, day after day, the drill went on.

On the first day of firing live shells at helium balloons released from the bridge, everyone not on watch clustered on the fantail to observe the proceedings.

Spracklin growled out of the corner of his mouth to his crew: "All right, you guys, there's an audience watching you, get on the ball."

All hands watched the bright-red helium balloon soar over the foremast.

The first shell left the *O'Bannon* rocking in the swells. All eyes were on the telltale track of the tracers. It was wide of its mark. The balloon rose higher. The watchers groaned.

The second shell was closer. The third was even closer. The

fourth ripped the balloon to shreds, and the boys on the fantail cheered and pounded each other on the shoulder.

But Lieutenant Philip and Chief Spracklin were far from satisfied. After the firing, drills were resumed. Ranging, loading, and simulated firing went on again and again until the weary men felt they would fall in their tracks on the next try. But Philip and Spracklin both knew what the green youngsters did not, that when it's your life or the enemy's in a split second, only perfection will decide the winner.

Chief Boatswain's Mate McGrath and his repair parties went over blueprints of the *O'Bannon*, learning all her secrets. They searched and found every bulkhead, wiring, fire hydrant, and steam cutoff. McGrath split his men into groups of eight and placed one forward, one midships, and one aft.

He told each repair party: "I want every man to know everything there is to know on this ship. I want you to be able to find every bulkhead, every valve, every piece of wiring, fire extinguisher, and every rivet in your own section—and God help you if you can't . . ."

Before the shakedown cruise was over, it wasn't unusual to overhear one of McGrath's men saying, ". . . And so I left Pete standing forward by the chief's quarters—you know, by the bulkhead with that unpainted rivet head about four inches from the deck . . ."

In the meantime Chief Fire Controlman James Bess and Fire Controlman First Class Willard C. Davidson learned that their crew consisted of several schoolboys, an oil salesman, a miner from West Virginia, and a schoolboy who volunteered in order to save his father, who was head of the local draft board, from handing him his draft notice over the dinner table.

From early morning until late at night Bess had them handling the intricate fire-control tools which keep in working order the delicate range computers, gun directors, and optics of the range finders; the wiring, the tiny gears and motors, and the massive calculators which make up the fire-control system of a ship.

15

These tools ranged from what looked to be an eyebrow tweezer to a huge fifteen-pound wrench.

Under Bess's patient direction they learned to compute their ship's speed, target speed, wind—both along and across the line of fire—the target's movements during the time of the flight of the projectile, and the difference in temperatures which influence the powder.

Again and again Bess went over the same problems. "Some night when a Jap bastard is pitching steel our way, you'll be damn glad you did this," he would tell them.

In the galley, Pappy Rowland took over the ship's supply of food. With his three other ship's cooks, he arranged menus for the officers' wardroom, chief's quarters, and the crew's mess, served cafeteria style.

In between drills tons of supplies, foodstuffs for Pappy Rowland's galley, engineering parts, and radio spares, were stored away. The crew, too, discovered that rust was a persistent enemy, and under the watchful eye of Boatswain McGrath, details were constantly chipping and painting the ship.

Slowly, almost imperceptibly, under the ceaseless drilling, the *O'Bannon* began to grow into a fighting unit. Comradeship grew daily. The wardroom became noisy with laughter. Nicknames replaced the formality of the first few days at sea. A sense of deep responsibility was acquired by the officers when they found that neither Wilkinson nor MacDonald interfered in their departments and both trusted them to handle the jobs assigned to them.

After a little more than three weeks the *O'Bannon* turned back to Boston.

The shakedown cruise was over.

2 WAR TOUCHES THE
O'BANNON

CHIEF GUNNER'S MATE SPRACKLIN was spinning a yarn.

He was sprawled on the rolling weather deck, his back against the bulkhead of the radio shack. Sitting next to him, chewing a match, was Chief Watertender Zimmerman.

It was a few minutes before midnight. The *O'Bannon*, long, slim, and compact, speared her way through the night leaving in her wake a trail of whispering foam. She was headed out to sea on an anti-submarine patrol.

The period allotted the shakedown cruise had been far from adequate, but Captain Wilkinson and Executive Officer Mac-Donald were not too discouraged. Both the green crew and the reserve officers had shown an excellent spirit and a willingness to learn; this they hoped would compensate for their lack of training.

Two hours after her arrival in Boston, orders had hurried the destroyer to Newport to pick up a load of torpedoes with new, brassy war heads. War was coming closer to the *O'Bannon* and her crew as she headed out into the Atlantic.

Up on the weather deck, Spracklin was saying:

"Well, we went into drydock, Zip, when the old man gets word that the *Von Tirpitz* is running around the Atlantic. That night he sent a message to Washington suggesting that his old can be sent out to get the raider. Here we are in drydock, afraid to sneeze for fear of busting a bulkhead and . . ."

He stopped. Someone was pounding along the deck. Like all veteran yarn spinners, Spracklin hated to be interrupted.

"Someone is in a hell of a hurry," he grumbled to Zimmerman. Unroe, panting and blowing, skidded to a stop in front of them. He was shouting:

"Get in the fireroom right away. Get the other boiler underway. This is the real thing—Convoy hit by subs—Message just coming in—"

He was interrupted by the hoarse klaxon of the general-quarters alarm.

Zimmerman leaped for the fireroom ladder. Without touching the rungs he slid down. Unroe followed, first dogging the hatch. As Zip's feet hit the steel plates the fireroom annunciator bell from the bridge clanged urgently and the iron arrow swung to Full Speed Ahead.

"This is no drill," he shouted to his crew. "It's the real thing."

In the darkened pilothouse Captain Wilkinson and MacDonald hovered over a large chart with a small pencil-flashlight. In one hand Wilkinson held the message which had been given to him a few minutes before.

"Looks like we'll reach them by daylight, Mac," Wilkinson said. "I hope we're in time to get a crack at one of them."

MacDonald nodded. The *O'Bannon* was starting to quiver now, eating up the darkness and the distance. The blowers were whining in a high pitch. Her stern was flat to the sea, boiling it astern.

MacDonald moved near the helmsman.

"Let her come over two-two-zero."

"Two-two-zero, sir. . . . On now, sir."

"Steady as she goes."

"Aye, aye, sir. Steady as she goes."

All through the night the *O'Bannon* raced at high speed to the aid of the ship under attack. It was just daylight when the lookout on the wing of the bridge called out: "Objects in the water dead ahead."

Both Wilkinson and MacDonald swept the sea with binoculars.

18

"Looks like half a lifeboat," said MacDonald.

Wilkinson cursed.

"Right ten degrees rudder. Steer for that lifeboat, Helmsman." He dropped his binoculars against his chest.

"Bodies out there too," he said shortly.

In a few minutes the *O'Bannon* passed the lifeboat. There was no need to stop. It was split in half. Bobbing up and down beside it in the swells were the bodies of several merchant seamen. One was just a torso. Over an area of several miles oil cans, crates, mattresses, smashed lifeboats, life rafts, and bodies littered the sea.

All day the *O'Bannon* combed the area for survivors. None was found. Late that afternoon another destroyer steamed up and by blinker light informed the *O'Bannon:*

"Have picked up two boatloads survivors. Rest believed dead."

Late that night Chief Radioman Padgett rushed a second urgent message to the bridge. Another ship in a convoy had been torpedoed, and the *O'Bannon* was ordered to the scene. It was in the early hours of the morning before she reached the area of the attack and started her cat-and-mouse search.

The destroyer hunted the U-boat all through the night, keeping tenaciously on the track of the undersea wolf.

The sea was heavy, and the *O'Bannon* rolled and pitched with the wild, irresponsible motion of all destroyers. On the bridge Wilkinson and his officers were forced to cling to the brass rail that circled the pilothouse, while the quartermaster cursed under his breath as he tried to get her to answer his commands.

In the chart room, Soundman First Class C. L. Conn, headset glued to his ears, listened intently to the sharp ping of his sound gear, searching for the sub. The constant ping-ping-ping filled the room like the plucked strings of an invisible banjo. Scarcely breathing, face grim, Chief Padgett hovered over Conn as the soundman slowly moved the dials in front of him.

For hours they searched without success.

Then at dawn subs struck again. The *O'Bannon* had just moved in to take her place on the flank of the convoy when three red rockets burst across the dull morning sky. Three more ships had been torpedoed—scattered merchantmen steaming in to take their positions.

The convoy had been attacked by a wolf pack. One ship seemed to disintegrate in a ball of flame. Another belched thick black smoke and in a few minutes settled down to become a raging inferno, fed by thousands of gallons of high-octane gasoline. Percussions from depth charges of other destroyers rumbled across the sea. One of the tankers was hit again and she exploded, turning the ocean into a solid sea of blazing oil.

Down in the *O'Bannon's* fireroom, the dull thuds of the exploding depth charges pounded with giant fists against the thin steel sides.

One boy cried: "We're hit!" And he moved toward the fireroom ladder.

Zimmerman grabbed him by the arm.

"Going for a walk?"

The boy began sobbing. "If they hit us we'll be caught like rats down here."

Zimmerman grinned and put a fatherly hand on the youngster's shoulder.

"Son, you're afraid? What the hell do you think I am?"

The boy was wide-eyed.

"Are you afraid, Chief?"

"Hell, I'm dirtying my pants right now, kid."

The boy took his still trembling hand off the ladder.

"I'm sorry," he said, "I lost my head." He moved back to his battle station and picked up a burner. There was a job to be done.

A few seconds later another spread of depth charges exploded —this time much nearer—and the concussion slammed against the *O'Bannon's* bulkhead. A bulb burst in its socket. Paint chips and dust filled the air. One of the firemen who had been topside came tumbling down the ladder.

"Gee, I just saw a couple of guys without heads floating around in the drink out there. The whole damn sea is burning."

Zimmerman threw a handful of oily waste at him.

20

"Forget it, kid, and get to work," he said quietly.

All that day the *O'Bannon* and her sister destroyers hunted the U-boats. The water boiled with the volcanic fury of exploding depth charges, but the subs had again escaped. The *O'Bannon* was ordered back to port for another escort assignment.

That night a member of the crew stopped MacDonald on deck. He grabbed the executive officer's arm.

"Please, sir, I want to be transferred. I don't want to be on a ship any more. I want to go ashore. I saw those bodies out there today. I saw the ships . . . I'm afraid to die . . . I have a wife . . ."

MacDonald looked closely at the boy. He was still wearing an inflated life jacket although General Quarters had been secured hours before. His eyes were red from crying. He was obviously badly frightened.

"Please, sir," he was whispering, ". . . please, sir."

The executive officer placed his hand on the boy's shoulder.

"There are a few hundred officers and men on this ship who would all love to go home right now and forget about war, son. But unfortunately we can't. There's a job to do and we must all do our share. If we don't fight for our country we won't have one to go back to. None of us wants to die, son . . . try and control yourself . . . we've got to stick it out . . ."

Raising his hand in a weak salute the boy walked away. MacDonald, chewing on an empty pipe, moved to the lifeline and went out into the blackness.

The *O'Bannon* was a tense ship that night.

The nightly pinochle games were forgotten. Some of the crew lay in the bunks without speaking. One boy quietly recited his Rosary, others thumbed their Bibles. For the first night since they left Boston the phonograph was silent.

In the fireroom two of the crew approached Zimmerman and Unroe.

"When we get hit what are the chances of getting out, Zip?" one asked.

Zimmerman shrugged his shoulders.

"It's over within a few minutes, isn't it?"

Zimmerman and Unroe both nodded.

"Thanks, Chief," one said as they turned away.

The feeling of fear swept through the ship. Lieutenant Pfeifer reported that some of the crew refused to remove their life jackets. Several boys, Boatswain McGrath said, were sleeping on the decks. They pleaded to be left there.

In their quarters the chiefs drank endless cups of dark coffee and listened to Unroe:

"These kids are like a bunch of lambs going to the slaughter-house. Here we got the best can in the fleet with all the fire power possible, the latest equipment, and what do they give us? A bunch of kids as green as shamrocks. Well, I'm damn glad my insurance is fixed so my old lady will get something."

Next day all chief petty officers were ordered to the bridge.

"We've got to keep on drilling them," Wilkinson told them. "Drill them and drill them and drill them. You can expect General Quarters any hour of the day or night."

Wilkinson's order was followed to the letter. The chiefs couldn't be satisfied. Assignments were done over and over again.

"When you can do it blindfolded, try it ten more times," they told the men in their departments.

Speed and accuracy were constantly demanded. In the fire-rooms, engine room, gun turrets, radio shack, the chiefs called for speed, speed . . . and more speed. There was no rest at night. After chow, classes were organized in the officers' quarters and the crew's quarters, and diagrams pasted on the bulk-heads. Questions were shot out suddenly, answers demanded the same way. More questions, more answers, more diagrams—and then permission to hit the sack.

General Quarters sounded day and night. To the weary boys it seemed as if they had just closed their eyes when the rasping yap . . . yap . . . yap would bring them rolling out of their bunks and stumbling in the darkness to their positions.

"Can't you give us just one night's sleep?" they pleaded as the days passed, but the chiefs just growled:

22

"Don't you know the Navy is saving your life this way?"

Under the relentless drilling the shock of the torpedoing wore off, but it was never forgotten. In the crew's quarters the nightly pinochle game was started again. "The Colonel," Joseph Oliver, seaman first class, a short, chubby boy from Alabama, continued to play "Rose of My Heart" until someone would throw a shoe at him, while Seaman First Class Eddie Goman picked up where he had left off describing his experiences as a coal miner in Wilkes-Barre.

At night crew members could always be found sitting in a circle around Spracklin as he sprawled out on the weather deck, spinning tall tales of the "old days on the four-pipers." The CPO never failed to draw a laugh. His favorite yarn was about the sailor who was chipping the hull of his ship with a hammer. It was a warm day and the seaman started to doze off—still chipping. Suddenly he heard a shout. It came from in front of his hammer. The startled seaman looked down right into the face of an angry fireman. He had chipped his way right through the paper-thin bulkhead into the fireroom.

One night, hearing the gale of laughter that followed one of Spracklin's yarns, MacDonald looked up at Wilkinson from a sheaf of papers.

"You know, Ed," he said, "I think those boys are coming around fine."

Wilkinson smiled. "Do you know what one of them told me tonight on deck, Mac? 'Captain,' he said, 'you know, this is a hell of a swell ship we got here.' "

Three weeks later found the *O'Bannon* headed for the West Coast. At Balboa Captain Wilkinson received his orders to join the Pacific Fleet. The first stop was to be Noumea, New Caledonia.

On the way out to the Pacific it was drill, drill, drill, more intense than ever. Day and night the klaxon blare of the general-quarters alarm sounded. Drills averaged at least five a day, sometimes lasting for three hours.

Finally, when it seemed as if this world of sleepless nights, irregular meals, wet clothes, and the constant, urgent blare of

General Quarters would never end, the *O'Bannon* reached Noumea.

A few weeks later, she headed out again to open sea. Her destination was Guadalcanal.

3 THE BATTLE OF GUADALCANAL

*Please inform every man of the force who so success-
fully assisted in reinforcing the brave men on Guadalcanal and
then magnificently and with eagerness became the sharp edge of
the sword which cut the enemy's throat, as follows: In your
brave night action I knew the odds were against you but also
felt it was the time which brave men and fine ships could be
called upon for their supreme effort. You more than justified my
confidence and expectations. You took from the enemy a toll of
strength far greater than your losses. I grieve with you for the
cherished comrades who gave their all and for the lost ships. The
names of those men and those ships will be enshrined in history
and the name of your force should be reserved for all time for
ships and men as ready as you have been for the highest patriotic
endeavor.*

—Vice Admiral Richmond K. Turner, USN

It was the early morning of November 12, 1942. The *O'Bannon* was slipping past the coast of Guadalcanal—past Koli
Point, where the green grass is as open as a race track; past
Aeola, where the heavy jungle grows right to the water's edge—
and finally sailed to the beach where the Marines had landed on
August 7, initiating America's first great offensive in the war in
the Pacific.

25

Executive Officer MacDonald, watching the rough coral coastline slip by, murmured to Quartermaster Gotschall, at the helm:

"Steady as she goes, Gotschall."

"Steady she is, sir," he echoed. There was a moment of silence in the pilothouse. Then the quartermaster cleared his throat.

"Gosh, Mr. MacDonald," he said, "this place looks as quiet as a grave. Where's all the shooting we've been hearing about? I guess I'll never believe a newspaper again. . . . Do you think we'll see any action, sir?"

MacDonald dropped the binoculars and let them jerk against his chest at the end of the lanyard. He stared at the blue-green mountain range towering into the brilliant tropical morning and then turned to the quartermaster.

"Gotschall," he said softly, "I think you'll get your belly full before we leave this place."

Despite the doubting quartermaster now squinting at the lush jungle as the *O'Bannon* slid by, Guadalcanal had seen plenty of action.

Not a day or an hour had passed without some action on land, sea, or air. The battle of Santa Cruz had been fought to a bloody and violent draw a few weeks before. The carrier *Hornet* had been lost. Our last one, the *Enterprise*—"the Big E"— was badly damaged. Our air forces were improving, but still the Tokyo Express steamed down from Rabaul and Bougainville to doggedly put ashore troops and supplies.

On November 7 in New Caledonia, the *O'Bannon* had joined four large transports and one cargo ship, together with the *Monssen* and the *Barton* and later the *Atlanta* and *Portland*, two light cruisers. The convoy, first to glide into "Sleepless Lagoon" since the battle of Santa Cruz, was under the command of Rear Admiral Daniel Callaghan, former aide to the President and known from captains down to the humblest messmen as "Uncle Dan."

It was 0530 when the forces anchored. Two officers who had the mid-watch were still lingering over hot coffee in the wardroom. On deck the fireroom hatch swung open. Zimmerman and Unroe stepped out. It had been thirty hours since they had tasted fresh air. Zimmerman wiped his grimy face and looked out across the lagoon to Guadalcanal.

"Christ," he said, half to himself, "what the hell are we going to do with this after the war is over?" He threw himself on deck and watched the heavy transports unload their supplies. Suddenly, the early morning quiet was shattered by a thunderclap. Zimmerman jumped.

"What the hell is that?" he asked Unroe, who was leaning on the lifeline.

The chief watertender pointed to a large waterspout just off the port side of one of the unloading ships.

"Shore batteries," he said. "They're trying to get that transport." Shell spurts began walking toward another transport.

A slim, powerful cruiser was entering the lagoon, a large "50" painted on her bow in white numerals.

"There's the *Helena*," Unroe said. "Isn't she a beauty? She'll take care of that Jap bastard."

The heavy cruiser cut her speed. Off Kokombona she let go with her heavy guns. Thunder rolled across the sea. Several boys raced out of passageways to the weather deck to watch.

"She's afire," someone shouted. But she wasn't. The *Helena* gunners had turned to rapid fire. Flames enveloped her from stem to stern. Gunner Spracklin, watching, growled to some of his gun crew:

"See that? Those guys know how to shoot."

The boys grinned. They knew Spracklin was secretly proud of the last gunnery scores.

In a few minutes the Jap gun was silenced and the *Helena* circled the transports, like a mother chick worrying about her brood.

At 1318 the Japs gave their reply. One of Chief Radioman Padgett's strikers rushed a message to the bridge. Wilkinson glanced at it, then snapped to MacDonald and Philip:

"Japs coming in. Sound General Quarters."

On the flagship, the new antiaircraft cruiser *Atlanta*, brilliantly colored signals mounted the flag hoist.

"Cease present operations," they read, "form disposition for antiaircraft."

Aboard the *O'Bannon*, General Quarters sounded across the water. The clang of other alarms could be heard plainly. The transports left their boats in the water, weighed their anchors, and lumbered out of the lagoon. On the bridge, Wilkinson scanned the sky with binoculars. He turned to MacDonald.

"Mac, you conn the ship. I'm going to tell the crew what's up."

Moving to the ship's loudspeaker, he said:

"Men, this is your captain. We expect an air raid very shortly. I want all hands to be on the alert and ready. That is all."

At 1405 the Japs came in. There were thirty-six torpedo Mitsubishi bombers stretching across the sky in neat triangles. The *O'Bannon* was tense. Every eye watched the planes as they crossed the volcanic mountain on Savo Island. Some skinned so low across the water, they seemed to dip beyond the horizon. Before they reached their torpedo-dropping range, signals fluttered on the flagship.

"Execute Turn Nine," the signalman reported to MacDonald.

"Left full rudder, steady her down on two-seven-oh."

"Steady on two-seven-oh," the helmsman echoed.

The *O'Bannon* heeled gently to her portside. The *Helena*, at the head of the column, opened fire. Aboard the *O'Bannon* a boy on one of the 20-mm.'s pushed his back against the steel brace of his gunner's harness. He gripped the handles of the gun. He cursed softly to himself. He had waited a long time for this moment. He remembered a telegram that had arrived the morning after Pearl Harbor. It was brief. It regretted that his brother had died in the attack. A buddy had written later, ". . . And when the Japs came over he was in the engine room." Yes, he had waited a long time.

On the bridge Wilkinson's orders crackled.

"Pick 'em up and knock 'em down . . . fire when ready."

The gunnery officer already had his guns trained on a group of nine bombers coming across the starboard bow. The antiaircraft guns chattered with one voice. The *O'Bannon* was still firing when the order came from the flagship to turn left 90 degrees.

"Left full rudder."

"Steady on course one-eight-oh."

"I'm steady on one-eight-oh, sir."

The second group of Jap planes began a run on the *O'Bannon's* porthand. They were less than 200 feet above the ship. The Jap pilot in the lead plane leaned out and shook his fist as he swung in. The machine gunners on the porthand opened fire. Tracers streaked through the air, hitting the plane in the belly. It burst into flame and exploded as it crashed into the sea. The second was hit in the tail. Desperately the pilot tried to climb, but the fluttering plane made a complete circle and plunged down, turning over and over like a wind-blown leaf. The third met a machine-gun burst head on. It exploded instantly. Bits of wing and tail drifted over the sea, some only a few hundred yards off the *O'Bannon's* port and starboard sides.

The pilot of a fourth plane was undoubtedly killed instantly, for his plane, untouched by flame, failed to pull out of its dive and sank immediately.

The raid ended as abruptly as it began. The gunner who had lost his brother at Pearl Harbor stood up in his harness and thumbed his nose at one of the burning planes.

"That's for my brother, you lousy bastards," he shouted.

Comments raced across the deck:

"Who said those guys were supermen?"

"Did you see the guy that blew up . . . just like a match box. . . ."

"I got the Jap that shook his fist . . . square midships."

The boys strutted about slapping each other on the shoulder.

The *O'Bannon* had accounted for four planes. None of the ships in the force had been hit except the *San Francisco*. A bomber, caught in a cross fire, crashed in a suicide dive on her secondary control station. The burning gasoline took the lives of thirty men and seriously injured Executive Officer Mark Crouter. The crews of the gun stations died at their posts rather than leave. They were still firing when the Jap crashed into the blazing muzzles of their guns.

In less than five minutes there was no trace of the battle. The

Japs had lost thirty-five out of thirty-six planes. The remaining one raced homeward with a Grumman fighter buzzing angrily on its tail.

Several bits of debris from the Jap planes were picked up by the *O'Bannon* for identification purposes. One was a life jacket worn by a Jap pilot. There was an American stamp on the collar. Part of it had been ripped away by machine-gun bullets, and the bloodstained stuffing began to fall out on the deck as it was hoisted aboard. One of the crew members stared at it. He bent over and drew his hand across the jacket.

"What do you know about that?" he said, holding up a bloody hand. "It's the same color as ours."

On the bridge Lieutenant Philip was enthusiastic about his gunners.

"First time under fire, Captain, and they got four," he boasted cheerfully to Wilkinson.

That afternoon the Japanese five- and six-inch guns on Kokombona opened up again and columns of water rose about the transports as they resumed unloading.

The *Helena* and a string of destroyers steamed off to deal with them. With her battery of ~~fifteen~~ *nine* eight-inch guns and the five-inchers of the destroyers *Barton* and *Shaw*, the Jap batteries were silenced. At one point the *Helena* found twenty-five Jap landing craft, which the enemy had failed to hide. Under her fire they blew up in clouds of splinters.

The rest of the day was uneventful. The *O'Bannon* and her sister destroyers hung on the outskirts of the transports.

It became cooler at dusk. In the west the sky was stained a blood-red as the sun set. The transports, completing their jobs of unloading, had formed in a column, preparing to retire.

It was necessary that they be out of "Sleepless Lagoon" before dark. A huge Jap task force was reported steaming toward Guadalcanal.

The Jap force was split into a giant V. A third column was perched at the northernmost point of the V. First information had identified the ships as:

1—Two Kongo battleships, one Tenyru-class cruiser, and six destroyers.

2—Five destroyers about 195 miles from Guadalcanal had joined up with one or two light Natori-class cruisers and four more destroyers.

3—Two small carriers and two destroyers, steaming south of New Georgia Island, 150 miles away.

Through Sealark Channel, between Florida and Guadalcanal, Rear Admiral Callaghan's tiny task force of thirteen ships headed east.

At 2000 General Quarters sounded throughout the *O'Bannon.* In his galley Pappy Rowland yelled:

"Get a-hopping!" and the messmen tore off their aprons and scrambled down the ladders to the magazines and handling room beneath the crew's quarters. Firemen and watertenders slid down the fireroom ladder, first dogging down the steel hatch cover. In the fireroom additional boilers were started. Valves were twisted. The thick flow of the black oil gushed into the roaring fireboxes. Throughout the ship Boatswain McGrath's damage control parties took their positions ready to battle flood and fire. Gunners poured into five-inch gun mounts and slammed the steel doors.

In the radio shack Chief Padgett readied his code books in a thick canvas sack, weighted with ballast, to be dropped over the side—just in case.

In his stateroom Lieutenant Ditto was dabbing cold water on his face when the general-quarters alarm went off. He jerked himself upright. The rasping noise pulsed in his brain. He thought of the day the *Langley,* with her cargo of fighter planes and pilots, got it. She was listing badly that morning when he reached the deck. In a few minutes he was in the water. He was picked up by a ship that was torpedoed an hour later. "Damn, that was a day," he thought, as he picked up his helmet and ran along the passageway. All the lights were out, he noticed, except the blue battle lamps. He reached the bridge and began fumbling for the ladder to the flying bridge at the base of the director. In the chart house he could hear Wilkinson barking an order to the engine room above the steady rasping of the alarm. He grinned to himself. The old man certainly is going to rip into those bastards tonight.

Along the deck below men were racing. He could hear the slamming of the gun-turret doors and the heavy fireroom hatches as the crew readied the ship for action.

On the flying bridge he could make out the still, intense faces of the men on the 20-mm. guns as he fumbled with his earphones. Impatiently he pushed the earphones under his helmet.

"Let's get going," he said quietly to the men around him. He pressed the button of the sound power phones.

"Bridge, this is secondary testing . . . testing."

"Test okay, secondary," a voice told him. He turned around and peered into the blackness. In the pilothouse Wilkinson turned to MacDonald.

"Okay, Mac, turn her off."

The executive officer pulled the switch of the general-quarters alarm. It stopped abruptly.

"That damn thing will drive a man out of his mind," Wilkinson said. There was silence on the bridge as both MacDonald and Wilkinson bent over the steel bridge chart table against the port bulkhead. Ensign John D. Creigh, communications officer, stood calm-faced under the TBS (Talk Between Ships) speaker at the entrance of the port wing of the bridge, ready to relay any orders from the flagship that might go unnoticed in the din of battle.

On either side of the quartermaster at the helm stood the engine-room talker and the captain's talker, human echoes that would repeat each command to the departments throughout the *O'Bannon*.

Wilkinson picked up his binoculars and swung open the hatch to the port bridge wing.

Through his glasses he could see the phosphorescent furrows of the faintly silhouetted ships as they swung into position to cover the retirement of the merchantmen. The column cleared the beach and soon met the choppy waters of the open sea. Wilkinson noted that only one damaged can and four small ships were guarding the vital transports as they swung south. He bit his lips. "If those Nips ever get at those ships . . ." His face was grim.

They moved through Sealark Channel, leaving the cumbersome transports behind, steaming to safety in New Caledonia. A signal light blinked in the night. "Close interval to five hundred yards," it said.

Wilkinson stepped into the pilothouse.

"Ahead one-third."

"Ahead one-third," the engine-room talker echoed. His voice sounded shrill in the silence.

Midnight, Friday the 13, Callaghan's forces approached Lengo Channel. The ships deployed into battle formation. The *O'Bannon* was fourth in the battle line of destroyers and cruisers. Leading the pack was the *Cushing*, followed by the *Laffey*, the *Sterret*, the *O'Bannon*, the *Helena*, the *San Francisco*, the *Portland*, the *Juneau*, the *Atlanta*, the *Aaron Ward*, the *Barton*, the *Monssen*, and the *Fletcher*.

The moon had set, the sky was overcast, the night pitch-black. The sea was smooth as a dull black mirror. A slight nine-knot breeze, blowing from the south-southeast, whispered through the ship's rigging.

Chief Yeoman Irvin Fahrbach took his position under the bridge chart table, ready to record the night's action. He tested his tiny blue-lens flashlight.

"Ready, Fahrbach?" Wilkinson peered down at him.

"Aye, aye, sir."

He opened his notebook and sat tailor fashion. In the dimness he looked like a brooding Buddha.

On the bridge of the *O'Bannon* there was silence. As the force steamed through the channel MacDonald said quietly to Wilkinson:

"Captain, I'll take the deck."

"Very well, Mac," Wilkinson answered.

There was silence again until the TBS loudspeaker (Talk Between Ships) came to life with Callaghan's deep, rich voice:

33

"Peter to Peter's boys: Stand by to execute turn."

And then: "Execute turn."

The single column of ships swung in the darkness at a 90-degree angle, entering Lengo Channel.

Through the bridge's port, MacDonald could see the phosphorescent wakes of his sister ships. Guadalcanal loomed dark and mysterious on the *O'Bannon's* porthand. Throughout the ship, in the firerooms, turrets, and handling room, the men who would see none of the action waited tautly at their stations. Those topside or aloft watched the open sea—waiting.

Over MacDonald's head Callaghan's voice boomed out through the loudspeaker:

"Let me know if you see anything."

Off Jap-held Tassafaronga, a bright, white light blinked. The lookout on the bridge called out:

"Aircraft with navigation lights dead ahead."

Overhead they could hear the faint drone of planes. Lieutenant Philip, peering through the darkness from his perch in the director, reported:

"Looks like a torpedo wake ahead, sir."

"Anybody else see it?"

"May be shallow water, Captain," MacDonald answered.

The lookout reported to Wilkinson:

"Contact! Targets sighted."

Suddenly the *Helena* over her TBS reported:

"Jen to Peter: I have enemy on starboard bow!"

"Peter to Jen": Callaghan replied in code. "Can you make them out? . . . How many?"

"Jen to Peter: There are several . . . can't make them out."

With that the TBS became chaotic with confusion. Voices tumbled out of the loudspeaker.

"Joseph to Peter: I have four ships in fanlike formation."

"Charles to Peter: I have ships on port bow."

"Jen to Peter: I have ten targets. Can I fire?"

"Peter to Jen: Go ahead."

A blinding Jap searchlight pierced the darkness. Its narrow shaft shot across the sea. It fastened itself on the force. With one

34

gigantic movement it swept the length of the column, tapping each ship with a rigid white finger, as if to say, "I see you . . . and you . . . and you . . ."

"Odd ships fire to the starboard; even ships fire to port. Commence firing." The voice of Admiral Callaghan was calm.

On the *O'Bannon* Wilkinson's order was brief. "Shift to portside . . . get that searchlight." The words had scarcely left his lips when the *O'Bannon's* five-inchers roared. She trembled with the concussion. Giant orange spears pierced the curtain of the night. Wilkinson shouted something but his voice was lost in the thunder. All ships in the column were ablaze with gun blasts.

In the director Lieutenant Philip saw the tracers of the *O'Bannon's* first salvo scar their way across the night. He saw the splashes of fire as the shell tore through the superstructure of a three-stack Tenyru-class cruiser. The second salvo roared over the hull of the cruiser, now burning fiercely, and caught a second Jap ship steaming up to join the battle. There was a burst of flame. The Jap was a roaring torch that circled crazily.

Several large flares exploded over the sea. They floated down slowly, throwing fantastic shadows about the water.

Out of the hard white light loomed an enormous silhouette. She moved across the sea like a sluggish monster.

Wilkinson, MacDonald, and Philip, glasses to their eyes, caught it at once. There was no doubt about it. She was a battleship. A Kongo. Huge. Later identified as the *Hiyei*, she bristled with the fire power of her fourteen-inchers. Next to her the destroyer was a pygmy. Although the Jap was in range it was impossible to fire her torpedoes; friend and foe looked alike in the blackness.

Wilkinson roared:

"Get on the battleship . . ."

The Kongo opened up with all her guns. Her salvos were directed at the cruisers turning to engage her. She ignored the *O'Bannon*—but not for long. The destroyer's guns blossomed flame. She rocked sharply, staggered, then continued to draw near her giant target. Hits exploded about the Kongo. Once she turned on a searchlight to examine this tiny enemy, but it was shot out in a second by the *O'Bannon's* gunners.

Fire broke out all over her. Her guns continued to stab at the zigzagging cruisers.

In the director Lieutenant Philip was talking to Bess in plot.

"What's your range now, Bess?"

"Two thousand yards."

"Bring it down . . . bring it down."

Bess brought it down to 1,500 yards. He heard the deafening roar of a salvo. Then Philip's voice again:

"Bring it down again."

"Are we hitting her, Lieutenant?"

"Yeah, bring her down, Bess, for Christ's sake will you bring her down . . ."

Sweat streamed off Bess's face in torrents. He could taste the salt on his lips. Furiously twisting the dials and knobs of his computer he set the range at 800 yards.

Another salvo.

"Bring her down, Bess."

Bess screamed:

"Goddamit! I got her on almost zero . . ."

"Okay, bring her on zero," said Philip calmly. "We're going alongside this guy."

Salvo after salvo roared away from the *O'Bannon*. Bess and his men, their faces almost green under the blue battle lights, waited. Suddenly the darkness burst apart, off the *O'Bannon's* portside. There was a tremendous roar. In the fire-control room, it bounced off the steel walls like a solid mass. It left ears ringing, as if from a heavy blow. The Kongo had burst into flame, battle masts and hull stark against the red sky.

"God, this is murder!" Bess heard Philip exclaim.

The battleship, a roaring fire midships, kept on her course. She bore down on the *Laffey*, crossing her bow by only a few feet.

Directly in front of the *O'Bannon*, the *Sterret* was hit. She swung about in a welter of spume. An explosion on her stern lit the interior of the *O'Bannon's* pilothouse like a huge electric light. From where he was standing MacDonald could see a gun mount fly through the air. The *Sterret* stopped dead in the water.

"All engines back full," MacDonald shouted.

The *O'Bannon* heeled over violently, shuddering and skidding on beam's end in the foaming sea. By less than thirty feet she cleared the blazing stern of the *Sterret*.

"Full ahead. . . . Come back to base course . . ."

The *O'Bannon* swung back into line. She was now the leading ship. The *Cushing*, *Laffey*, and *Sterret* had disappeared—sunk or badly damaged.

Out of the darkness, blazing from bow to stern, but still mighty with destructive power, again loomed the *Hiyei*. She opened fire. A salvo roared over the *O'Bannon's* foremast. To Lieutenant Ditto and the men at the 20-mm. guns on the flying bridge, it sounded like an express train moving across the sky.

The *O'Bannon* immediately engaged her. They dueled at 1,500 yards. Destroyer against battleship. Peashooters against 14-inch cannons. David against Goliath.

Twisting, leaping forward for a lightning thrust, maneuvering, feinting, she traded blows with her giant foe. Five-inch fireballs tore the Kongo's forecastle to tattered steel. One side was aglow from the inferno within. Her plates looked as if they had been painted with a brush dipped in flame. Wilkinson's orders cracked like a bullwhip about the bridge.

"Right full rudder . . . Course two-two-five . . . All engines full . . ."

The *O'Bannon* wheeled about, her after guns hammered at the Kongo. More explosions on the Jap. The destroyer's blowers were in a high whine. A wall of water boiled furiously about her fantail. Green water covered her forecastle. The battleship couldn't depress her guns fast enough. The *O'Bannon* bore in again. Her rifles thundered. The recoil of the salvo pushed her back on her haunches. Every rivet quivered. She raked her enemy with thunder and flame. An enormous ball of fire leaped to the sky, covering the Kongo's pagoda tower with a cloak of flame. Explosions followed. Debris flew through the air. So near was the *O'Bannon* fragments of molten steel from the battleship showered about her decks.

Wounded seriously, the sea monster turned away in the darkness. The strip of green sea which divided the ships widened more and more. The *O'Bannon*, tendrils of smoke curling from the panting mouths of her guns, paused.

The sea was now a wild confusion of flame and thunder. The Battle of Guadalcanal was no longer an organized naval fight; it had turned into a savage barroom brawl with all lights out and no holds barred.

To young Cianca on the *O'Bannon's* flying bridge, it seemed as if he had stepped through the gates of hell and peeped at the inferno within.

Off to the starboard, the *Portland* had begun a duel with a destroyer of the Hibiki class. At close range they slugged each other with screaming salvos. Then the *Portland's* fire touched off the magazines of the Jap ship. Before the boy's horrified eyes the Jap blew up in a gust of pure white flame, ripping in half. As she disappeared in the furiously bubbling water, her boilers hissed like an aroused giant snake.

All about the *O'Bannon* there were gun flashes and fiercely burning ships—both American and Japanese.

Off the *O'Bannon's* porthand, the cruiser *Helena* had swung about and was charging at a destroyer, all her guns raging. The Jap ship seemed to leap out of the sea like a thing alive. A search-light was turned on briefly and Cianca could see her fantail disappearing in the foam.

But towering above all the other ships, moving about the sea like a stricken giant searching for refuge from a relentless enemy, was the blazing Kongo battleship. She was spotted by the *Helena*, who moved in with salvo fire. The Kongo's guns answered as she tried to match shell for shell. Cianca could see balls of fire dancing about her rigging.

He heard a shouted command. The *O'Bannon* had charged again into the center of the still raging battle.

At 0154 Admiral Callaghan ordered:

"Cease firing."

This command was lost in the thunder of the battle which rose again in all its fury. The *Cushing*, badly wounded but still afloat, had engaged the *Hiyei*. There was an explosion on the

Cushing but she continued to fire. The Kongo made a hard left rudder and moved back into the path of the *O'Bannon*.

"Get on the battleship . . . Torpedo tubes set for a spread . . . Fire when you bear . . ."

The *Hiyei* moved closer. She was less than 1,800 yards off the destroyer's starboard bow, her guns silent. With a loud swish the steel fish left the *O'Bannon's* tubes. In the fireroom "Pop" Popino marked a large piece of white cardboard as he counted loudly:

"One—two—three—I love you and you love me . . ."

The smell of cordite, sucked in through the blowers, filled the fireroom.

On the bridge they sensed the thuds, the splashes. One—two—three—away. Off the side trails of sea fire fanned out toward the target. The Kongo crept closer, her high pagoda tower outlined against the sky.

Three dull explosions jarred the sea with muffled violence.

"A hit," someone said.

The *Hiyei* was now dead in the water. A crimson torch crept up her side. It grew as high as her masthead, where it mushroomed into a pure white ball of fire.

Five ships were now blazing astern of the *O'Bannon*. Less than 1,500 yards away, a light Jap cruiser that had been dueling with the *Aaron Ward* rolled on its side and sank.

The *Barton* bubbled in a fountain of flame from a direct hit. She split in half and with a metallic scream of twisted plates sank within two minutes. Her screws, dripping in the glare of the gun flashes, were still turning.

The *San Francisco* had engaged the *Hiyei* and was pouring shells into the blazing hull. Suddenly off her starboard side a heavy Jap cruiser and destroyer steamed in to cross her bow. The *Helena* asked:

"From Jen to Peter: We have targets, can we fire?"

Callaghan answered:

"Peter to Jen: What kind? We want the big fellows."

The words had just died away on the TBS speaker when the enemy cruiser opened fire. The first salvo scored. The shells tore the *San Francisco* bridge structure into twisted, smoldering steel. Captain Cassin Young and Commander Mark Crouter were killed instantly. Another shell smashed the conning tower to kill Rear Admiral Callaghan. A third exploded in Battery Two, killing everyone there. The *San Francisco's* guns kept firing. In a few seconds the Jap destroyer blew up like a mound of powder touched by a match. The explosion shook the sea with violent, deafening roars.

Several hits were scored on the cruiser. She retired. The *O'Bannon* swung north barely missing the sinking *Laffey*. Hundreds of shouting men were swimming about in the water.

"*Laffey* . . . help . . . *Laffey* . . ."

"Get those bastards, O'B . . ."

"Throw us some life jackets . . . life jackets . . ."

Crew members topside on the *O'Bannon* ripped off their jackets and tossed them over the side. They had gone a short distance when a terrific explosion lifted the *O'Bannon* clear out of the water. Men were tossed about like chips.

In the fireroom bulkheads bulged and retracted. The floor plates looked as if they were about to burst. Paint scales and dust from a thousand hidden crevices filled the air. All lights went out. A steam gauge snapped and live steam hissed through the room. Zimmerman, his hands twisting two blower throttles, felt himself lifted high in the air. He hung there spread-eagled. Slowly, by inches, he managed to free his arms. Both felt as if they had been wrung from his body.

Shouts filled the darkness.

"Lights . . . turn on the lights . . . watch that gauge . . . smoke watch says we're smoking . . . where's Zip?"

Finally James H. Joiner, a young electrician's mate, plunged his hand into the master switchbox and located the damaged circuit breaker. He plugged in a wire. One false move—a brush against the wrong wire—and the boy would have been electrocuted on the spot. Lights blinked. Fleming thrust his hand through the steam and shut it off. Boiled flesh peeled from his arm.

In the handling room Pappy Rowland had just opened his box

40

of Copenhagen snuff. The explosion tossed him to the deck. Seaman Cianca, who had been ordered to help load the shells to the gun turrets when the firing became heavy, was slammed against the bulkhead, the wind pushed from his lungs by a 75-pound five-inch shell. The lights went out and a frightened messman began screaming.

"We're hit . . . Pappy, we're hit."

Rowland, picking himself up, shouted:

"If you don't stop that screaming, I'll stuff a shell down your gullet."

Cianca fumbled for the battle light; turned it on. In the dull blue light, Pappy was examining the empty snuff tin.

"Damn those Japs," he growled. Moving over to the loading hoist, he tried the electric button. It was dead.

"Go topside and see what the hell is doing," he ordered Cianca.

Grabbing his life jacket, the seaman clambered up the ladder. On deck he climbed to the flying bridge. As he reached his station a Jap cruiser of the Tenyru class turned on its searchlight and caught the *O'Bannon* in its beam. He heard the cry:

"Fire four . . . five . . ."

He smelled the brassy cordite; could hear the splash as the tin fish knifed toward the Jap cruiser. The seconds passed. Cianca felt frozen to the deck. A dull thud. A flash of flame. He could see the Jap spin about in the frenzy of her death agony. She stopped dead; split in half, and sank. Her bow plunged down into the sea as if seeking a quick end. Her searchlight was still on. As she went down the finger of light pointed the way to the muddy bottom, fathoms below.

On the bridge a clock was torn from a bulkhead and smashed into a hundred pieces at Fahrbach's feet. Wilkinson and MacDonald were hurled across the pilothouse. The quartermaster, clinging desperately to the helm, felt an invisible hand snap his head back.

Again the *O'Bannon* lifted out of the water, settled back with a tremendous smack. Her bow plunged deep. The quartermaster spun the helm, but it was dead.

"Lost control, sir," he cried. He reached down and yanked the emergency alarm lever. There was no ring. The ship had lost power.

"All power lost, sir . . ."

As if in answer the *O'Bannon* lifted her nose out of the sea. Green water cascaded off her bow from as far aft as Number One. Shuddering, she resumed her course. She had regained her power.

Repair parties reported to Wilkinson.

"Everything all right in the after engines. . . . Everything all right in the forward fireroom. . . . Everything all right in the after fireroom. . . ."

The *O'Bannon* picked up speed. It was agreed the explosion was probably the boilers or depth charges of a sunken ship.

"Let's go and hunt some more targets, Mac," Wilkinson ordered.

Less than three thousand yards away, despite her serious damage, a Fubuki destroyer let go with two torpedoes and several salvos. The fire of the explosions on the Jap set off the fury again. The whole area blazed with cross fire. The *Aaron Ward* engaged a Natori light cruiser and sunk it at 3,000 yards. Star shells burst over the sea illuminating the battle and revealing the burning *Hiyei* circling slowly in the water. Her guns were silent. The *O'Bannon* moved in for the kill.

"Ready torpedo tubes . . . fire one . . . fire two . . . fire three . . ."

More explosions rolled across the flaming sea. The belly of the Kongo was cherry red. She was dead in the water. The *O'Bannon* poured in salvo after salvo. The Kongo drifted away slowly.

Several star shells burst over the *Monssen* dead ahead. A Jap cruiser hit her with a salvo that blew her Number One turret to bits.

It was 0250.

The *Fletcher*, all guns thundering, raced to head off a Maya-type cruiser 600 yards off her bow. The Jap ship blew up with an ear-splitting roar.

A flashlight blinked aboard the *San Francisco*, her only form

42

of communication left, as she told of the death of her commanding officer.

"Captain Cassin Young, Rear Admiral Callaghan, Crouter killed. We are badly damaged. Please transfer all doctors and pharmacist mates with medical supplies."

Nine ships were now burning fiercely. Fed by her magazines, a Náchi cruiser exploded. She was followed almost immediately by one of the Tenyru class.

In the pilothouse Wilkinson called the *Helena* to report he was entering Lengo Channel.

"Pass the word for Doc Dunham to be prepared to board the Frisco with medical supplies," Wilkinson ordered. Throughout the ship the loudspeaker blared:

"Dr. Dunham report to bridge . . . Dr. Dunham report to bridge."

From his battle station in the officer's wardroom, Dr. Dunham hurried to the bridge. Briefly Captain Wilkinson gave him his instructions. In a few minutes a whaleboat was cast off with the physician and two pharmacist's mates.

The *O'Bannon* headed for home. It was 0400. Her baptism had been a Niagara of fire.

As they steamed away from the hulks still smoldering on the sea, some of the crew stumbled on deck. Exhausted, they threw themselves on the deck and slept. Lieutenant Philip entered the chart room. He was pale, with deep, sootlike smudges of exhaustion under his eyes. He lighted a cigarette and inhaled deeply.

"It was murder, Captain," he said. "It was murder. When we hit that battleship she just turned into a torch. And I know we got a cruiser, too."

He turned to MacDonald:

"Have you ever seen anything like this, sir?"

The executive officer shook his head:

"I think it will go down as one of the bloodiest battles in naval history. It may even be the turning point of the war."

The three looked at each other in silence.

43

Chief Torpedoman Braun climbed to the bridge. He carried a jagged chunk of an eight-inch shell.

"I got a souvenir for you, Captain," he said with a grin.

Wilkinson examined it.

"Where did you get it, Braun?"

The torpedoman scratched his head.

"When one of that battleship's salvos went off this thing came sailing over and went between the legs of one of my torpedomen. It took part of his pants leg off but didn't scratch him. It must have hit the torpedo mount because the whole thing is damaged. I found it a few minutes ago stuck about six inches in the deck."

At 0800 the *O'Bannon* was ordered to leave the force in a feint direction to send a message back to Com-So-Pac describing the condition of the ships and giving a brief outline of the night's battle.

At 1300 she rejoined the force and swung into line:

Wilkinson, scanning the ships, turned to MacDonald:

"That's strange, Mac, the *Juneau* is missing."

Over the TBS loudspeaker he asked the *Helena:*

"Michael to Jen: Where is *Juneau?*"

There was a moment of silence. Then:

"Jen to Michael: *Juneau* died at 1018."

Wilkinson, eyes bleak, moved to the chart table.

As the force steamed back to Tulagi, Chief Radioman Padgett stood on deck and thought of home—particularly of his six-year-old daughter Carol. He fingered the cheap, metal identification bracelet on his wrist. Carol had given it to him the night before he left. It had taken all of her carefully hoarded two hundred and fifty-six pennies. "If you wear it all the time, Daddy," she had told him, "you'll never get lost. All they have to do is read the name and address on your bracelet and they can send you right back to me."

He walked into the steaming radio shack. He sat down at his polished steel table and wrote:

Dearest Alberta:

By this time you have found out from the papers what happened on this date. You will also know the *O'Bannon* came through with flying colors. It was our baptism of fire. Now we know what war is really like. We all realize that we are up against a cruel and inhuman foe who will stop at nothing to gain their ends of conquest. That foe must be exterminated or we shall never have a lasting peace.

A number of Americans will die in this process. That is why you have received this letter. Trust no rumors, take nothing for granted until the Navy Department has confirmed it.

Remember one thing, I shall love you always, Alberta. My life with you has been full and overflowing with happiness. Keep your chin up. Pray for me.

Love,
Pat

He slipped the letter into an envelope. On it he wrote: "To Mrs. Alberta Padgett." He slid it into his drawer. Later that night he told Guess about the letter. The first-class radioman nodded:

"Funny, I've written the same kind of letter to my wife. Let's do this, Pat. If anything happens to one of us, the other will deliver the letter—if he can go back for it. Agreed?"

They shook hands.

In the fire control room Spracklin was telling Bess:

"Now I know one thing."

"What's that, Sprack?"

"Well, dammit, I'm finished telling stories. How the hell could I tell one that can top last night?"

When the *O'Bannon* reached port it was late in the afternoon. A boat was sent over to the base to pick up Dr. Dunham. Back on the ship he reported to Captain Wilkinson. His hand shook as he puffed on a cigarette.

"What happened over there, Doc?" MacDonald asked.

The physician shook his head. They saw his haggard, sleepless face tighten. They watched him as he spoke.

"The Frisco was a death ship," he said flatly. "A death ship. The men wounded and stunned were lying about the decks. There were dead men in all compartments. The bridge was a shambles of human parts. The first thing I saw on deck was an arm with a finger pointing at me. Bodies were blown into the superstructure. She had been hit by everything. The emergency sick bay midships was piled high with seriously wounded. I saw the Frisco doctor. He just said: 'Thank God, man, you're here.' I went to work at once. For hours I seemed to be splashing through pools of blood on deck. I did everything, operate, dress wounds, blood plasma . . ."

He stood up and shrugged his shoulders. "I cursed myself for only having two hands."

He nodded and walked out.

4 MUNDA BOMBARDMENT

THE *O'BANNON* WAS steaming her way back to her Tulagi anchorage after escorting General Vandegrift's battle-weary Marines to Australia. It was several weeks after the Battle of Guadalcanal. In the pilothouse, humming to himself as he stared out a port, Executive Officer MacDonald suddenly stopped and turned to Captain Wilkinson.

"Gosh, Ed," he said, "tonight will be Christmas Eve!"

Wilkinson, poring over a chart, looked up puzzled.

"Christmas," he said as if he had heard a familiar but not recognizable word, "Christmas Eve . . . gosh, you're right, Mac."

He straightened up and rubbed a hand across his cheek.

"Let's see now," he mumbled, "what can we have . . ."

He paused and then snapped his fingers.

"I got it . . . Mac, pass the word along to Rowland to prepare a special menu for the ship and let's see if Guess will write a Christmas poem for the *O'Bannon* . . . He's good at that sort of thing."

And so that night George Guess read the *O'Bannon's* Christmas poem. Guess was a husky, good-looking boy with curly blond hair and a fullback's shoulders. He was a radioman first class—and in the opinion of Chief Padgett, who should know, he was "slightly terrific." George, who hailed from Louisville, Kentucky, had been a newspaperman in civilian life and had served in city rooms from Kentucky to Trenton, New Jersey. Besides radio he had one other love—writing poems.

47

As he looked down on the grinning officers—some toying with the Christmas presents they had given each other: a polished screw driver, a monkey wrench with a piece of red ribbon— Guess wished he was back on watch in the radio shack.

The wardroom was thick with cigarette smoke. The dishes had been cleared, the last of the chicken had long disappeared. Pappy's three-layer sponge cake with the red and green trimmings had dissolved into a few crumbs which were now rapidly vanishing into Lieutenant Pfeifer's mouth.

Executive Officer MacDonald rapped for order.

"Quiet, gentlemen, Radioman Guess has a Christmas poem to be read." He nodded to Guess. The radioman cleared his throat and began to read:

South Pacific Christmas on "Mike" O'Bannon

'Twas the night before Christmas, and all through the ship,
Not a vent blower sounded, not a shower did drip;
While 'mongst all the crew members, so safe in their bunks,
Danced visions of liquors, and of ice cream in hunks;
The Captain was up on the bridge in his robe,
The Radioman tapped with a voltmeter probe;
And all was in silence as, mystic, the night
Descended like curtain to shut out the light.

The night crept along, and the mid-watch came on,
The lookouts were wide awake, hoping ere dawn,
That jolly Saint Nick would soon ride on the air
Bringing Merry Noel Greetings from the folks "over there";
The Bos'n wants clothes for his cute "Brisbane Babe"—
The Engineer for a new bearing does crave;
They all had their minds set on certain small things
Which only Saint Nick on his yearly trip brings.

Suddenly—the lookout—he shouted, "What ho!"
And there, crost the face of the moon—but lo!
'Twas a sleigh and some reindeer, and a broad smiling face
Beamed on "Mike" O'Bannon, shouting cheer and good grace.
'Twas the friend of our long-ago childhood years
Bringing loads of good words for us, bags of good cheers;

48

The reindeer descended, and with grace did they plop,
Thru' the black of the night on our turret top.

Saint Nicholas made his way up to the bridge,
To bring the men up there good Christmas porridge;
He unslung his bag, and he brought out his books,
At which men on the bridge would steal surreptitious looks;
He called off their names, and he named them their deeds,
Both the bad and the good, with their races and creeds;
He strode to the microphone, the button did poke,
And then through the dark of the night thus he spoke:

"You have suffered a lot, and have proved that you're men,
You have lived, you have loved, and you hope to again;
In the hearts of all men who pray daily for peace,
You have given new faith, and on life a new lease;
The people at home are all thinking of you
And trusting that soon they will see you all, too;
Let us then do our best to make all the world free,
In the year of our Lord nineteen and forty-three.
Merry Christmas and Best Wishes to all."

The wardroom stamped and cheered when Guess finished.

"Very good, Guess," Captain Wilkinson said. "Be sure and put that up on the bulletin board."

In Plot, Chief Fire Controlman Bess was deep in thought when Chief Gunner's Mate Carl Settlemyer walked in. He and Bess were close friends.

"Got a cigar?"

"A few. Why? What's up?"

"Dig them up and get ready to hold your hat," Settlemyer warned, " 'cause you've been a daddy for a couple of weeks now. I got a letter from home. It's a boy."

Bess sat stunned. Then he let out a roar. He grabbed Settlemyer by the hand and pumped it up and down. He stopped suddenly.

"Wait a minute," he said. "How the hell did you know it before me?"

The chief grinned. "Your telegram has probably been misplaced. Your wife figured that would happen so she asked 'em at home to pass the word. Now where in the hell are those cigars?"

Bess unlocked a drawer of his desk. He pulled out a box of cigars.

"Been saving these," he said. "Thought I might need them for the happy event." He stuffed a handful in Settlemyer's shirt pocket.

Up in the pilothouse Wilkinson watched the water slip by without actually seeing it. The Captain was thinking of his wife and small son. He wondered if Richard would like the trains he had bought. He grinned as he remembered the day he addressed the package. It was so hot the perspiration from his hands blurred the ink—as he wrote, "Merry Christmas from Dad."

A week later found the O'Bannon in Noumea. The entire month of December had been a quiet one for the naval forces patrolling the Solomon area. Both sides, it seemed, were preparing for the next major battle. On Guadalcanal General Patch's army lines were well formed between the muddy Matanikau River and the Tassafaronga River, twelve miles west of Henderson Airfield. The Japs were operating from their main base, twenty-five miles away at Cape Esperance. Admiral Halsey was forced to use his few remaining destroyers and cruisers to convoy supplies to the troops on Guadalcanal. Day and night a steady stream of ships, loaded with high octane gas and bombs, shuttled back and forth between New Hebrides and Guadalcanal. For the men of the O'Bannon it was a twenty-four-hour-a-day job with little sleep and irregular meals.

The Tokyo Express, derailed the night of November 12, was again roaring down the Slot from Rabaul and Bougainville and landing supplies that were sent by trucks overland to Jap troops within the front lines.

Early in January planes reported a large airfield was being hacked out of the coconut forest at Munda, on New Georgia. From Kolombangara Island, Japanese forces were sending supplies down to Munda by destroyers. Once the airfield was completed, waves of Japanese bombers would be able to take off from Munda and in one hour reach Guadalcanal to bomb vital transports. To hold Guadalcanal it was important that Munda be knocked out.

It was against this background that the *O'Bannon* reached Tulagi early in January. She was ordered to join up with her sister destroyer, the *Fletcher*, and the cruisers *Helena*, *Honolulu*, and *Nashville*. That very night she was to take part in the bombardment of Munda Airfield.

The force was under the command of Rear Admiral Ainsworth —the destroyers under capable hard-hitting Captain Robert Briscoe.

Earlier in the day Ainsworth had informed all captains that "Black Cat" pilots were to be used. Completely fearless, the Cat pilots flew their lumbering Catalinas, painted entirely black, over enemy installations, spotting the bombardment for the force. To meet up with a highly maneuverable Zero might be fatal. Sometimes, bored with just chanting "Up 500 . . . left . . . 200 . . . right . . . 400 . . ." they would drop dozens of pop bottles. The weird screaming never failed to send the Japs burrowing in their foxholes and praying to their ancestors. Once Tokyo Rose indignantly called it a "new barbaric American horror weapon."

At 1700 the force slid out of Tulagi and headed up the Slot. Night fell quickly. The sky was dark and overcast. Passing showers slashed across the *O'Bannon's* decks. In a single column the ships moved through Lengo Channel. Ainsworth's flagship, the *Nashville;* the *Honolulu* and the *Helena;* with the *O'Bannon* and the *Fletcher* screening.

At 2230 a Black Cat droned overhead, headed for Munda. The showers ended. The moon rose, veiled in a mist and peeping at the edge of a single motionless thundercloud. Less than an hour later it was completely obscured. The sky was clear, however, and the stars came out to quiver with diamond fire.

An hour passed. There was silence throughout the ship. Except for a quiet command no one spoke in the pilothouse. Rendova passed on the starboard, and then Bannyetta Point. Astern on the *Nashville* a signal light blinked.

"Open distance for bombardment," the lookout called.

A Black Cat pilot droning high above the field began chattering:

"Angel testing . . . testing . . . what a night for romance . . . Hope you guys are ready to pitch . . . I wish I had a chocolate soda . . . nice and gooey with three scoops of ice-cream . . ."

In his steaming radio shack Chief Padgett growled:

"For God's sake stop it, will ya?"

In the gun mounts the men stood ready to slam home the five-inchers and the powder. In the handling room below, Pappy Rowland and his messmen, surrounded by enough shells and tins of powder to blow them and the *O'Bannon* into fragments, had nothing to do but wait. To pass the time, between chewing at pinches of Copenhagen, Pappy told his gang about his postwar plans. At home he owned a car—"a long green job with plenty of chrome"—and it was the apple of his eye.

". . . And after this war is over," he said, leaning against the hydraulic hoist, "I'm going to get in that car and just ride around and around."

"Hey, Pappy," one of the messmen asked, "what happens if we get hit down here by a shore battery?"

The CPO scowled.

"We won't know what hit us. And, don't change the subject. Now about that car . . ."

In bombardments split-second timing is absolutely necessary, and each captain knew exactly what minute his ship would swing into bombarding position; when his guns would range the target, and when he would swing about and retire.

In the pilothouse Wilkinson intently watched the luminous dial of his stopwatch. . . . The hand moved from minute to minute . . . 0008 . . . 0009. . . . At 0010 the *Nashville*, abreast of Munda, turned right rudder. At 0012 her guns belched flame. A thundering salvo shattered the still night. The bombardment of Munda Airfield had begun.

The Black Cat reported:

"On the mark . . . on the mark . . ."

Another salvo stabbed fingers of flame toward the dark outline of the island.

Black Cat: "Not too good . . . come up 500 . . ."

The *Nashville* moved along the target. Meanwhile, on the *O'Bannon*, crew members not required by their jobs to remain below were given special permission by Wilkinson to go topside to see the bombarding.

As each ship reached the bombardment point she joined in the rapid fire. In the blackness it seemed as if fiery hoses were pouring streams of molten steel on the island. The boys on the deck of the *O'Bannon* watched, awestruck.

The shadowy shoreline became livid with flame. The thunder of the bombardment line blasted the night apart. An enormous pillar of white flame outreached previous fires: a magazine.

At 0022 the *Nashville* stopped firing. She swung about, foam boiling under her stern. Several bright fires flared up on the island. But the Japs—caught asleep—had awakened. Shore batteries barked back. Tracers, red and green, rose out of the blackness, and with high-diving arches reached for the ships. They missed, wide of their mark.

In the blackness a curious phenomenon occurred. On the *Fletcher* a lookout reported:

"Large ship off the port bow." By blinker she signaled the *O'Bannon:*

"Enemy ship off our bow. We will engage."

She swung, hard left rudder, but there was no ship. The *Fletcher* hunted back and forth, but there was no sign of the mystery ship. She had vanished as if swallowed by the night.

The *Helena* moved into position. Her first salvo was short.

Black Cat: "Come on, sweetheart . . . up a little, baby . . . try 200."

The second salvo hit the target square. A huge column of flame, outlining the black jungle, rose higher and higher. Zeros on the runway, probably. Orange daggers from the *Helena's* forward guns stabbed the velvet night. More fires on the Munda airfield. A second hit. The waters of Kula Gulf burned red with the reflections.

The Black Cat called: "Well done."

The *Helena* stopped firing and moved through the darkness. It was 0040. The *Fletcher* and the *O'Bannon* took their positions. On the bridge Wilkinson called to his executive officer:

"I'm in position now, Mac."

MacDonald asked Philip in the director:

"Stand by, George, are you on bearing?"

"All set, sir."

"All set, Captain," MacDonald reported.

"Commence firing."

The *O'Bannon's* five-inchers thundered, all with one voice. She rocked with the recoil. On the wings of the bridge Wilkinson felt the hot breath of his guns. "This is more like it," he thought. "Give those little Jap bastards a taste of their own medicine." The even voice of the Black Cat pilot interrupted his thoughts.

"Bring her over . . . you're hitting in the water."

In the handling room Pappy's messmen, naked torsos gleaming like ebony in the dim light of the battle lamps, fed shells and powder into the slow-moving hoist. The air hung like a wet, suffocating blanket. The gray steel walls were beaded with the sticky heat. To talk was an effort. Keep those shells and powder tins going topside. That was all that mattered.

In the gun mounts it was first the shell, then the powder . . . Stand back . . . Fire . . . Kick the casing out.

The *O'Bannon's* five-inch rifles slammed again.

Black Cat: "Bull's eye."

On the island more fires broke out. A gasoline depot exploded. A fiery lily rose in the darkness, orange petals spreading across the sky.

At 0102 Wilkinson ordered:

"Cease firing."

A complete and utter silence filled Kula Gulf.

"That last one was over home plate," the Black Cat reported. "I'm heading back. So long."

MacDonald swept the island with his binoculars. Munda was a roaring torch.

"All ahead full," he ordered.

"All ahead full," his talker echoed.

The *O'Bannon* began to eat up the darkness. She quivered as Zimmerman and his gang in the fireroom let the rich, thick oil gush in the fireboxes, and the turbines churned with increased power.

Above them, exhausted crew members flung themselves on deck. The high-pitched whine of the blowers lulled them to sleep. At dawn Grumman fighters from Henderson joined the force as the ships passed the squat, mountainous Russell Islands. At 0900 flags fluttered up and down on the flagship.

"Cut her down. Twenty-eight knots." MacDonald ordered.

"Cut her down. Twenty-eight knots."

MacDonald joined Wilkinson on the port wing of the flying bridge. The executive officer, eyes half closed against the glare of the morning sun on the water, silently packed his pipe.

"Planes approaching," the lookout yelled. Both Wilkinson and MacDonald grabbed their glasses. Swinging off Cape Hunter, in a neat diamond formation, were ten Aichi-99 dive bombers, the sun on their wings. Through his glasses Wilkinson could clearly see the red ball of Japan. MacDonald leaped into the pilothouse and threw the general-quarters switch. The harsh alarm rang over the ship. Men ran to their battle stations. On the wing, flying fantail, and deck, bridge gunners strapped on their helmets and slid into the harness of the 20-mm. guns.

Five thousand feet up the first three planes slipped into a dive, plunging downward to the *O'Bannon*. All guns opened up. The first plane released its bomb. It hurtled down, growing larger and larger. Several of the men on deck threw themselves flat. Screaming like a banshee, it exploded fifty yards off the *O'Bannon's* bow. A column of gray water erupted out of the sea. The plane started to pull out of its dive. It hesitated as if stopped by an invisible hand. Ribbons of fire and thick black smoke poured from the engine. Out of control, its pilot either dead or wounded, it turned on its back and plunged into the sea. The gunners shouted and pounded each other on their backs.

The second plane dove. The 20-mm.'s chattered. Halfway

down it disintegrated, showering flaming debris about the sea.

A third plane crashed off the *Helena*. A 250-pound bomb exploded a short distance from the *Nashville* without doing any damage. The Grumman fighters darted in and out the Jap formation.

One Aichi suicide-dived into the force but was blasted to flaming fragments. Jap planes were falling out of the sky like autumn leaves. The Grummans were having a field day. One plane escaped and slid low and fast toward the *O'Bannon*. Tracers from the destroyer's deck rose to meet it. Again and again they hit, but still it kept on. Less than 100 yards off the destroyer's starboard side it curved over and plunged into the sea. Another followed, but swung sharply about to come astern of the *Honolulu*, to strafe her decks. A Grumman pounced on it and the Jap fell into the sea leaving a train of black, greasy smoke. The remaining Aichis fled into the sun with Grummans spitting tracers about their tails.

Rear Admiral Ainsworth, over the TBS, ordered:

"Proceed to base."

Swinging into line, the *Fletcher* and *O'Bannon* on either side, the column headed southward for Tulagi. Soon the planes were out of sight, but the men on the fantail could still see the black column of smoke, hanging in the air, left by the last Aichi. It would stay there until the morning breeze dissipated it.

On the way back the *Nashville* ordered the *O'Bannon* by semaphore:

"Investigate two objects off port quarter of *Helena*."

Swinging about, the officers on the bridge could see two men clinging to a piece of wreckage. Japs.

"Stand by to pick up survivors."

The *O'Bannon* slowed down, and Boatswain McGrath threw lifelines over the side and rigged up a Jacob's ladder. The two men, now easily identified as aviators, brushed away the lines. One man looked badly wounded. Again and again McGrath threw the lines over.

"Grab 'em, you monkeys," he yelled. One Jap called back in

Japanese but refused to grab the line. They were now only a few yards off the destroyer's side.

MacDonald ordered a whaleboat lowered. Jumping in the bow he leaned out to grab one of the men.

Snarling in Japanese, the aviator reached down inside his suit and yanked out a pistol. MacDonald, hanging halfway out of the boat, tried to strike it from his hand. He missed. The Jap pointed the pistol at the executive officer's head. He pressed the trigger. There was a dull click. The cartridge had failed to explode.

On deck an alert gunner swung a machine gun around. It chattered. The aviator's head melted into a bloody pulp. Before his body sank MacDonald grabbed the pistol. Another man pulled the wounded Jap into the lifeboat. He was brought on board and Dr. Dunham ripped away his suit. He was badly wounded in the side and died an hour later.

In the pilothouse Wilkinson and MacDonald examined the Jap's gun. It was a 27-caliber pistol. The Captain held up the bullet that had nearly killed his executive officer. He pointed to the deep dent made by the firing pin.

"I guess we have an angel sitting on our foremast, Mac," he said.

Two days later in Espiritu Santo Captain Wilkinson received orders detaching him as Captain of the *O'Bannon* and ordering him to report to the commanding officer at an advanced Pacific base.

That same afternoon he said good-by to his ship and to the men gathered on the forecastle. He read his formal orders, then said:

"Your new captain will be Mr. MacDonald." He turned to his executive officer, who unrolled a sheaf of papers and read his appointment as Captain of the *O'Bannon*.

Both men shook hands. Then Wilkinson turned to the crew and officers.

"I wish I could stay with you," he said, "because I am confident that you men are going to make the *O'Bannon* a ship that will be remembered. Good luck and God bless you."

He saluted and walked down the quarterdeck to the gang-way. As he came to a corner, he turned to look at the ship for the last time, then disappeared.

On the *O'Bannon*, Lieutenant George Philip, Jr., was appointed executive officer. His job as gunnery officer was taken over by Lieutenant William Simmons, with Ensign John Creigh still communications officer.

5 BOMBARDMENT OF VILA–STANMORE

THE *O'BANNON* WAS Slot-running again, headed for the bombardment of Vila–Stanmore Plantation on Kolombangara. Reports had reached headquarters that morning of a landing of several hundred Japanese troops and guns of unknown strength. They occupied Vila–Stanmore Plantation, which was divided by the Vila River. Stanmore Plantation was on the west bank; Vila on the east. In the past two weeks Jap planes from Vila–Stanmore had heavily bombed Henderson Field as many as eight times in one night. Reconnaissance planes reported a line of supply barges strung across Diamond Narrows headed for Vila–Stanmore. MacDonald remembered the description by Rear Admiral Ainsworth that afternoon at the conference on the *Nashville.*

"They were loaded down to the gunwales with men and ammunition crawling across to Vila like a line of beetles."

Tonight Ainsworth's ships were on their way to bombard these troops and supplies.

The *O'Bannon* headed the column. Five thousand yards in her rear, MacDonald could see the phosphorescent curve of the *Nicholas'* bow wave. On either side were the *Nashville,* flying Ainsworth's flag, and the *Helena.*

Tonight's mission was dangerous. The *O'Bannon,* on entering Kula Gulf, was to plunge in alone, sweeping the sea for enemy ships. In the narrow gulf there was no maneuvering room. A

Jap task force coming down from the north, from either Rabaul or Bougainville, could easily box the *O'Bannon* in and destroy her. Her orders were not to awaken enemy suspicion after her sweep by returning farther south than halfway to Visu Visu. There she was to take a position off Waugh Rock to cover the firing line and—MacDonald smiled grimly at the word—"prevent" any enemy units from coming down from the north. As in the first Munda bombardment, Black Cats were to be used for spotting gunfire.

The sun set. The sea became opaque and heavy as molten lead. In a second darkness fell. MacDonald moved into the pilothouse. He walked over to the ship's loudspeaker. Since Captain Wilkinson left the *O'Bannon*, MacDonald had made it a nightly habit of talking to the crew.

"All hands, this is your captain. Tonight we are going to bombard Vila airdrome on Kolombangara Island. At the present time the Japs are in possession of all the surrounding land. We may see action tonight but no word has been received regarding surface ships. All hands will be called to General Quarters at 2130. Between now and then obtain as much rest as possible. When you are called to your battle stations, proceed quietly. Do not show any lights. Take as much water as you can carry. That is all."

He turned to Ensign Creigh:

"John, I'm going to rest here until 2130. Please call me then."

"Aye, aye, sir."

He settled in his armchair on the bridge and dozed. The radio loudspeakers now tuned onto the airplane circuits caught the low hum of propellers. On the canvas covers of the metal flag-bags on the bridge, men tried to sleep. In the fireroom, boys off watch slept oblivious to the continuous roar of the fireboxes.

The steady pulse of the *O'Bannon's* screws, the hiss of the bow wave, the whine of the blowers, combined to draw a soothing quiet about the pilothouse.

At 2130 Creigh wakened his captain. General Quarters was sounded. All stations reported to the bridge.

"Control reports manned . . . torpedo reports manned . . .

repair parties report manned . . . engineering department reports manned and ready . . ."

Chief Yoeman Fahrbach, notebook, pencil, and flashlight in hand, entered the pilothouse. He quietly took his position under the chart table where he would be out of the way but yet able to record the minute-by-minute action.

The *O'Bannon* was ready.

A rain squall came up, hiding the force now steaming through the sea at about twenty-six knots.

Two hours from the target, at 0114, the *O'Bannon's* lookout reported:

"Planes on porthand sighted. Bearing two-seven-oh, elevation ten degrees."

MacDonald leaped out to the wing of the bridge with his binoculars. They were two-engine bombers with white-tipped wings, carrying bright running lights. Signal lights blinked on one plane. Again and again she repeated the letter "U"—two dots and a dash. They swung lower, crossing the destroyer's bow.

The planes circled the force, flashing their signals. The force ignored them, knifing through the squall. After an hour the planes flew off toward Vila, still ignorant of the ships' identification.

The ships were at the entrance of the gulf. Sasanboki, low and sprawling, was outlined on the horizon off the *O'Bannon's* portside. Tunguilili Point soon appeared on the starboard. The destroyer entered the gulf—alone.

The shore seemed close now. Lookouts, straining their eyes, could make out the dark blob of Kolombangara. At half speed the *O'Bannon* cautiously felt her way through the darkness. The bridge was silent. It was a desperate, throat-catching moment. At such a range they were easy prey for Jap shore batteries. A Jap task force, sneaking down from the north, could blow the *O'Bannon* to splintered wreckage. Now and then MacDonald gave a quiet command.

"Steady on base course."

"Steady on base course, sir."

It seemed as if a century had pressed itself into those moments.

61

There were no stabbing flashes of flame, no blasting roar of hurtling salvos. Just silence.

At 0328 the sweep had been completed. MacDonald ordered: "Left full rudder."

"Left full rudder, sir," his talker repeated. The *O'Bannon* heeled to her port. Quivering with increased power she circled the advancing cruisers and took her position off Waugh Rock.

She was alone. One destroyer against anything the Japanese might choose to send down through the darkness of the Slot. The *O'Bannon* was tense. No one spoke. In the pilothouse, Mac-Donald felt his breath come a bit quicker; sometimes almost unexpectedly. His glasses swept the darkness. On both wings of the bridge his officers were doing the same; their only sound was small scraping noises as they moved across the rubber mat. There was no need to caution the lookouts. From their posts they were straining red-rimmed eyes, ready to cry out at the first sign of danger.

The silence was so heavy that Chief Gunner's Mate Spracklin, who was checking the men in the gun mounts, walked on tiptoe across the steel deck.

In the handling room, magazines, firerooms, and engine rooms, men imprisoned in the belly of the ship leaned against bulkheads waiting to leap to their stations. Even Pappy Rowland was silent as he stood by the ammunition hoist in the handling room, his eyes darting from man to man as he chewed snuff.

Out in the blackness Ainsworth's ships moved into position. Over the TBS on the *O'Bannon's* bridge came the words:

"Commence firing."

So abrupt was the command that MacDonald jumped, every nerve in his body quivering.

The bombardment started. It was 0338. Through their glasses and from the comments of the spotting Black Cat pilot pouring out of the TBS loudspeaker, the men followed the progress of the bombardment.

On the flying bridge, Lieutenant Ditto could feel rivulets of perspiration roll off his forehead. On the wing of the bridge,

Seaman Louis Cianca suddenly found his mouth had gone dry. His heart slowed down from its trip-hammer beat. Throughout the ship taut nerves relaxed.

The *Nashville's* guns fired first. Thunder rolled across the gulf.

Black Cat: "Come on, baby, bring 'em down. You can do better than that."

Another salvo slammed out through the blackness. Flames flickered, then rose higher on the island.

Black Cat: "Right in the breadbasket, baby!"

The *Nashville's* shells walked up and down her target, her guns never stopping. Pin points of fire grew larger and larger on the coastline. Once a supply depot exploded and a mounting pillar of flame climbed higher and higher. Through his glasses MacDonald saw six salvos of the *Nashville,* alone at one time, hanging in the air like racing comets.

"Damn good shooting," he commented to control.

The Black Cat was enthusiastic:

"That got it . . . you're hot tonight . . . that one was right across the plate . . . Oh! Oh, baby . . . a little low that time . . . up 200 . . . that's it . . . come on . . . who's next? . . ."

A Jap antiaircraft gun sent up a shower of tracers. The Black Cat said coldly:

"Get a ladder, ya Jap bastard."

At 0402 the *Helena* took her position on the bombardment line. Her first salvo blew up an ammunition dump. The towering flames were pure white. The boys on the deck cheered. In the last month the men on the *O'Bannon* had grown attached to the giant cruiser. In the chiefs' clubs on Tulagi and in New Caledonia more than one fight had been settled by Chief Spracklin's fists when the crack, "Glamour Girl," was passed.

Each ship fired for about twenty minutes. The night quivered and shook like warm jelly. The island blossomed with smoky orange balls.

The *DeHaven* and the *Radford* followed in line. A large building was hit. Fire silhouetted the framework. Suddenly it blew up in one huge gust of fire.

Black Cat: "That's wonderful. Now I'll send the boys a present." He dropped a 500-pound bomb.

All ships, after the last salvo, moved off in a single column. Behind them, as they pulled out of the gulf, the coastline was coated with a reddish haze, while intermittent white and orange columns of flame sprang up. One of the salvos had hit a Jap oil tanker which exploded, sending up clouds of oily black smoke and fire.

The *O'Bannon* left her solitary post and took her screening position off the cruisers. The moon had come out, but it was just a watery yellow disc, now and then obscured by lacelike curtains of cloud.

At 0505 a lookout reported to MacDonald.

"Plane sighted."

A large parachute flare exploded the next instant off the destroyer's bow. The *O'Bannon* requested permission from the flagship to open fire.

"Whippet to Beagle: Shall I fire on bogies?"

"Beagle to Whippet: Fire at will."

But before the *O'Bannon* could fire, Ainsworth ordered:

"Beagle to all ships: Turn."

The force swept into a furious rain squall. Overhead could be heard the angry droning of the Jap bombers.

"Beagle to all ships: Turn."

The column entered another squall. Again:

"Beagle to all ships: Turn."

Nature favored Ainsworth's force that night. Squall after squall appeared. As the ships emerged from one, Rear Admiral Ainsworth zigzagged them into another. At 0530 a large Jap twin-engine bomber swooped down out of the rain clouds and engaged the *O'Bannon*. She dived so low MacDonald could see the men in the plane.

"Get on him!" he shouted. But the 20-mm.'s were already firing. Tracers poked at the bomber like Fourth-of-July sparklers. He soared off into the mist. One ship now reported over the TBS:

"Terrier to Beagle: Enemy force of six ships contacted."

"Beagle to all ships: Execute Turn."

64

Again they were befriended by a rainstorm. Contact was lost with the Jap force.

A half-hour later, as they emerged from the rain the *O'Bannon* lookout sighted a large Jap bomber waiting for them. Before he could drop a stick of bombs all the ships opened fire. The Jap dogged in and out of the heavy clouds, wool-black puff balls of ack-ack fire bursting about him. He dove into one large cloud-bank. A second later there was a violent thunderclap. The cloud-bank turned a dull red. The bomber fell flaming into the sea. It burned steadily and soon disintegrated. At 0600 the other Jap planes returned to their base.

At 0720 the lookout called announcing American planes.

Fighter planes from Henderson Field had arrived to protect the force on their way back to the Tulagi base.

6 DOUBLE BOMBARDMENT OF MUNDA AND VILA-STANMORE

THE ONLY BREAK in the monotonous day had been when the *O'Bannon* moved alongside the stern of the supply ship, the *Aludra*. One seaman shouted:

"Anybody from Texas?"

"Yeah, hello," was the answer from two of the Texans aboard the destroyer.

"Look out, you guys, here it comes." A shower of candy and cake rained down on the *O'Bannon's* deck. Now, throughout the ship boys were munching on caramels, plain chocolate, fruit cake, and crackers. In the wardroom Dr. Dunham made ready a supply of castor oil.

Sitting alone in the pilothouse, Captain MacDonald clicked on the radio. He felt hot and irritable. The *O'Bannon* was hanging "on the hook," rocking gently in the swells. There were no awnings on the ship, and the decks were scorching. He listened to the radio's static for a moment, then turned it off. He still remembered the remark made by Quartermaster Gotschall a few hours before. The boy had asked:

"When do you think we'll be relieved, Captain?"

"Maybe in three or four days, Gotschall."

The quartermaster shook his head.

"I guess if we live four days we'll live fifteen."

The Captain sighed. It seemed a century had passed since they left Boston eight months before. He wondered what it would be like to be back in New York, say in a night club; in a well-lighted room, hearing the laughter of other people, the clink of ice—when had he last seen ice?—in highball glasses, seeing a cigarette girl passing among the tables, selling cigarettes and those long-legged dolls and animals.

He leaned over and again turned on the radio. From the frequency he saw it was Radio Tokyo. Tinny jazz records were being played. Then through the static he could hear the mellow voice of Bing Crosby's record, "I'm Dreaming of a White Christmas." The song ended abruptly. A flurry of drum beats followed. A man's voice spoke. MacDonald listened. The speech was for the poor misguided boys who were fighting the war for someone else. For their information the great Japanese Imperial Air Force had sunk four destroyers and a large cruiser last night off Munda. The cowardly Americans had sneaked in to bombard the Japanese positions but were driven off with great losses . . .

MacDonald snapped off the radio. God, he thought, how can the Japs be so infernally stupid.

Someone stepped into the pilothouse. It was his executive officer, Philip.

"The gig's waiting to take you over to the Admiral's conference, Captain," he said.

"Thanks, George," MacDonald got swiftly to his feet. As he walked out into the glare of the sun he wondered what was in store for them tonight.

It was two hours before MacDonald returned. In the wardroom he outlined the plan to his officers. It was another bombardment—this time a daring double-barreled one. One group would bombard Vila, the other Munda.

Despite the previous bombardments, Jap slave labor had put both Munda and Vila back in use. Planes from Henderson Field had delivered more than eighty attacks against Munda, but the Japs would repair the field within forty-eight hours. The battle of the Bismarck Sea had stopped the Japanese from reinforcing their garrisons on Lae and Salamaua, but Munda and Vila Airfields were still receiving an unusually large amount of men and

67

supplies and had to be destroyed at once. The *O'Bannon* was to join the Munda group with the *Nicholas, Fletcher,* and *Radford* under Captain Briscoe. The Vila group under Rear Admiral Aaron S. Merrill would include the cruisers *Montpelier, Cleveland, Denver,* together with the destroyers *Conway, Waller,* and *Coney.* Black Cats would spot as usual.

The *O'Bannon* and her sisters slid out of Tulagi. Munda lay over 190 miles to the north. It was a bright sunny day. As the afternoon wore on speed was increased. Under the new speed the *O'Bannon* trembled. Her blowers whined with a high pitch as air was sucked down into the engine room.

The afternoon was as clear as a bell. The sky was a startling blue, its evenness marred by only a few whisps of cloud, riding the breeze.

Darkness fell as they cleared the crowded, humpbacked islands of the Russells. At 2200 the Munda detachments split. The forces had been undetected by planes. The Japs might be in for a surprise again. Steaming up the Slot MacDonald gave his nightly "cannonside chat." General Quarters had been sounded and battle lamps turned on. Ports and hatches were dogged, battle ports sealed, hatches drawn. Except for the hum of the engines there was silence.

"All hands, this is your captain. We are going once again to bombard Munda Airfield, in conjunction with our cruiser friends who will hit Vila. We have no information that any task force will oppose us. However, this may be a hazardous operation. Wear your life jackets. If you are captured all you are required to do is give your name and rating. Do not tell what ship you are from or what you were doing. Silence is golden."

MacDonald went back to the wheelhouse and slumped in his chair. The bridge was silent. Down below he could hear the faint rumble of the pulsing turbines. He wondered what those Jap cruisers were doing out there. They would be fools to attack a superior force such as we had tonight. Probably lie in wait until the bombardment opens. Oh, well, we were ready for them.

At 0101 a dull explosion rumbled across the sea.

68

"Guns firing on starboard hand. Explosions," the lookout cried.

"The Vila group has probably met some cruisers, Captain," Philip said as MacDonald grabbed his glasses. He could see a bright orange fire, then another and another. Someone was hit. Flares exploded about the sky, drifting down to the sea like giant candles. Brightly colored tracers shot conelike in the air. The Japs were really trying to get that Black Cat tonight.

The TBS coughed into life.

"I am turning in to bombardment course. We will fire when ready."

"Bridge to director—Bill, we will carry out the planned operations. Let me know when you are ready . . ."

In the director Lieutenant Simmons squinted through the range finder. The gun mounts swung about.

"Director to bridge. We are ready."

"Commence firing."

Simmons pressed the firing key. The ship heaved with the recoil. Down the mounts empty shell casings clattered to the deck. Another range. Again the deafening salvo. Fire blossomed on the island. The Black Cat pilot broke in.

"Good shooting down there . . . there go some more of Tojo's boys flying around—without parachutes or planes." He then asked:

"Who's pitching down there?" In the radio shack Padgett asked:

"Butch to Angel: Good strikes?"

"Good work, Butch, keep them coming. Many fires down here."

The O'Bannon finished her time on the bombardment line and moved away. The other ships followed in rapid order. Across the rolling land masses they could hear the rumbling of the battle between the Vila group and the Jap cruisers. Gun flashes and flickering tracers could be seen clearly.

The bombardment of Munda finished, the destroyers rendezvoused. Suddenly a shore battery opened up and shells splashed about the zigzagging ships. Captain Briscoe ordered:

"Spike to Butch: Take care of that gun."

The *O'Bannon* spun about, whipping the sea to a white froth. The gun had been located by the Black Cat on Ilangana Point. Her first salvo silenced the Jap battery.

"Bull's eye, Butch," the Cat called.

"Bridge to director: Good work."

Turning, the *O'Bannon* raced to join her sisters.

The explosion heard earlier on the bridge of the *O'Bannon* was a 500-foot Jap cruiser bursting into flames off Vila–Stanmore. It took a spread of torpedoes from the *Waller* which split it in half. A remaining Jap cruiser turned tail and fled. In the meantime the bombardment continued. Ammunition dumps, coastal batteries, and barracks were blown sky high.

At 0150 the force retired to join the destroyers steaming toward Tulagi. Both targets were ablaze. In the vicinity of Munda's airfield a tall pillar of fire was straining to reach the sky. Several other smaller fires pin-pointed the blackness.

There was no rest for the weary men of the tin-can fleet. Late that afternoon, after spending a quiet few hours on the hook in anchorage, the *O'Bannon*, *Nicholas*, *DeHaven*, and *Radford* were ordered to join a "coconut shoot" against Jap positions around Kokombona Village. Before the ships took off a whaleboat pulled alongside and discharged a young Marine artillery officer who would act as spotter.

He was immediately invited down to the wardroom for a snack. He touched the clean white tablecloth almost in awe. He took a sip of coffee and closed his eyes.

"Coffee," he mumbled. "Real coffee. Don't wake me up." Between mouthfuls of chicken he described the bloody fighting on Guadalcanal. He had been on the island since the invasion on August 7. His body was ravaged with malaria and dengue fever. Most of the time he and his men had lived on moldy rice and scraps of meat. Even brilliant plummaged cockatoos were shot and thrown into a stew pot.

"This shoot today is going to be something *I'm* going to really enjoy," he said.

"Why?" someone asked.

He inhaled deeply on a cigarette.

"Yesterday we found two Marines in a ravine. They were part of a patrol. They weren't very nice when the Japs got through."

The rest of the day was spent blasting the Jap position. From the bridge the men could see the little bandy-legged men run for their foxholes. "That's what I like to see, Captain," the Marine said softly.

As the destroyers turned to head back for their nightly run up the Slot after firing several hundred rounds of shells, a blinker light on shore signaled "Very effective."

Before they left for that night's mission MacDonald and his officers said good-by to Doctor Dunham, who had been transferred. Lieutenant Robert C. Manchester reported as the *O'Bannon's* new doctor. He was a powerfully built man, blackened by the sun, with finely chiseled features that looked carved out of a block of mahogany by a careful workman. His thick black hair, cropped so close that it resembled a scalp lock, soon won him the name of "Tecumseh."

For her next few weeks the *O'Bannon* settled down to the routine of riding the Slot, submarine patrols, bombardments, and daily air raids.

One day, passing Quartermaster Gotschall on the deck, Captain MacDonald stopped him.

"Do you think you're seeing enough action, Gotschall?"

The quartermaster wearily rubbed a hand across his forehead.

"Captain," he said, "I'm just about ready to go back to that farm."

7 BATTLE OF THE SUBMARINE

WEEK AFTER WEEK the *O'Bannon* sailed each afternoon from Tulagi to sweep the Slot for enemy shipping. Sunset usually found her with the *Nicholas, Fletcher, Radford,* or *DeHaven,* steaming off the Russell Islands, where on February 21 she covered our landings which failed to encounter any enemy opposition. Daily Jap planes would zoom over the column, strafing and bombing. Occasionally a spear of tracers from the destroyers would stab a Jap and send him plunging down like a falling comet. Each night Captain MacDonald gave his "cannonside chat." Once he told the crew:

"Men, this is your captain. Tonight we're going up the Slot again. So far we have not received any information as to any Jap force coming down. However, there is a possibility that we might meet up with some barges. If we do I am sure you men can give them a royal reception, fitting for the honorable sons of heaven. General Quarters will be sounded the same time. Take canteens of water to your battle stations in case we have to stop and greet some Jap barges. That is all."

A heavy-set gunner's mate, moving across the deck, turned to a shipmate and said:

"I don't think they give the skipper the right dope."

"Why?" asked his buddy.

"Hell," he said, "they never tell him those barges are Kongo class."

General Quarters usually was sounded at 2100, and the men stood at their battle stations until 0800 or 1000 the next morning. Shadowy silhouettes of Jap-held islands became familiar landmarks on these lonely nightly sweeps. The black, irregular, volcanic coastline slid past them night after night. Each night brought them the unchanging panorama of dark sky, glossy black sea, and endless silent jungles edged with faint pencil lines of surf.

With decks cleared for action and every man at his battle station, the destroyer steamed past the low-backboned New Georgia mountains and Kolombangara's perfect cone to peer into the blackness of Kula Gulf.

Each night tense apprehension of what might be ahead surged upward like a tide. Men seldom spoke as they approached the area where Jap task-force units might come hurtling out of the night to mangle the tiny tin-can fleet.

Jap scouting planes lurked overhead in the clouds and would drop float lights that bobbed about the ships giving the scene a garish Hollywood effect.

Even on the trip back there was no relaxing of nerves that shrieked for rest.

Dawn brought back enemy planes. The lookout would report:

"Planes over starboard bow. . . . They are enemy planes . . ."

The 20-mm.'s would start chattering. Tracers, no longer sparkling and twinkling in the dull dawn, reached for the planes. They would heel over. Dive. Geysers of sea water rising about them. Then a yell as American planes appeared.

Fighters from Henderson. The Japs never stayed long. Climbing quickly into the sun they would speed back to Bougainville.

Bombardments were the only thing to relieve the tense, monotonous days. Bivouacs, supply areas, and airfields on Munda, New Georgia, Cape Esperance, and Kolombangara were subjected to intense shelling by the destroyers. Other nights they screened slow-moving mine layers placing their deadly eggs in enemy anchorages.

73

It was one of the nights on the way back to Tulagi that the *O'Bannon* sank a submarine and created the legend that today is told from the chief's club in Noumea to the bar in the Royal Hawaiian Hotel.

It was a pitch-black night. The *O'Bannon* was screening the force as it slid through the glossy waters of the Slot.

Captain MacDonald was napping in his armchair, head resting in the palm of one hand. The men were just black, shapeless mounds sleeping on the deck, against the torpedo mounts, and on the flag bags. In the sound room Soundman Conn listened wearily to the eternal ping-ping-ping of his sound gear. Suddenly he stiffened.

"Bridge!" he shouted. "Contact. Bearing two-six-zero. Check bearings."

MacDonald woke with a start. Nerves jangling, he was on his feet and alert before Conn had finished.

He asked for the routine check for a possible friendly sub.

Hands clasped over his headset, Conn was shouting the sub bearings. His husky voice rang about the bridge. Both Philip and Creigh, tense and alert, were at MacDonald's side. The Captain bent over a chart, a shaded light throwing a dull glow in front of him.

After Conn's first alarm MacDonald turned to the TBS speaker and said:

"Jeff to Mike: We think we have enemy ship. Range 500, bearing two-seven-zero."

The loudspeaker immediately replied:

"Mike to Jeff: Investigate. Attack if enemy target."

MacDonald turned to the helmsman:

"Right full rudder . . . all ahead full."

The *O'Bannon* swung starboard from the force, creaming the sea about her. She buried her stern deep, spun around and charged into the night. MacDonald pressed his face against an open port. He could feel the increased pulsing of the ship. She was alive now, vibrant. It seemed as if someone had shaken her and cried: "Wake up, *O'Bannon* . . . get on your feet . . . there is an enemy out there . . ."

74

"John," MacDonald snapped, "make sure Conn is sweeping the whole area."

In the chart house Philip bent over a squared paper on which he was plotting the course of the sub. The heat of the day, shut in by the darkening of the ship for action, choked the air.

Nice game, MacDonald thought, as he peered through the port into the blackness. Two deadly enemies shut up in a black box, tiptoeing about each other. Both armed with guns. Both out to kill. The loser gets death.

Suddenly his eyes caught a dim outline—the sub.

"There it is," he shouted, "dead ahead. Stand by to commence firing. Stand by to fire depth charges."

"Have you a solution?" he asked Bess, acting control officer that night.

"I have, Captain."

He turned to the helmsman.

"Come left . . . come left . . . more . . . steady . . . steady."

Lieutenant Philip, on the port wing of the bridge, shouted:

"Turn on that searchlight." The raw, white light caught two numerals, 28, on the submarine's bow. She was a big one. More than 750 tons, MacDonald noted, about 300 feet. J-class type.

"Conn, give me a bearing," MacDonald ordered.

"He bears two-eight-zero." Conn's voice was eager.

"Come around to two-eight-zero," MacDonald ordered the helmsman. He could feel the ship quiver with the vibrations of her propeller going astern.

"He bears two-nine-zero, sir," Conn reported.

"Come over to two-nine-zero."

"Two-nine-zero, sir," the helmsman echoed.

"God, we can hit her with a stone, Captain," Bess cried.

"Commence firing."

All of the destroyer's five-inchers slammed. The crew of the sub could be seen racing about the deck. They were small men dressed in dark shorts. Dinky blue hats bobbed on their heads.

The *O'Bannon* charged straight ahead. She bore down on the stricken undersea raider. A shower of flares shot up from the destroyer's deck. The sub's conning tower had been sheared off.

The *O'Bannon* passed within a few feet. Depth charges arched off her fantail. All straddled the sub. They lifted the undersea craft out of the water, only to savagely plunge her back.

And then it happened.

The crew was lined up along the lifeline, cheering. Here was sweet and deadly revenge for all those night runs up the Slot, for the sleepless days and nights of patrols, the attack and run tactics by Jap bombers. Suddenly one of the boys grabbed a shipmate.

"Come on!" he cried.

He rushed down the deck, half dragging his buddy. They reached the spud locker.

"Grab an end." The other had caught on. Bombardment by potatoes. Small, hard little potatoes—like pebbles. They rushed to the deck with the crate between them.

The sub was settling slowly. Jap seamen were pouring out of the gaping hole of the damaged conning tower. MacDonald swung his ship around in a wide circle. Now she was closing in for the final blow.

When they moved close to deliver the *coup de grâce,* a score of yelling seamen were lined up, waiting. Each had a fistful of potatoes—ammunition.

"Left rudder . . . more . . ."

The *O'Bannon* was circling the sinking sub. In the flickering glow of the dying flares Jap faces turned upward. Then the *O'Bannon's* crew went into action. Before the depth charges left her racks they let go. Potatoes flew through the air.

"Hey, catch this . . ."

"Watch me groove this one . . ."

"Strike one, monkey . . ."

The Jap seamen ducked. Little meaty balls bounced off their bodies and the sub's decks. Japs began diving in the sea, potatoes splashing about them.

One sailor remembered a 20-mm. gun that was being stripped down on the portside aft. Some of the parts were stacked at its mount. In a few minutes he was distributing nuts, bolts, and miscellaneous parts.

One of the Japs climbing on deck looked to be an officer. The sailor pulled back his arm. A thick, heavy nut flew through the air. The Jap officer was about to jump over the side. The nut caught him square. He tumbled off the deck. Nuts, bolts, machine-gun parts and Navy potatoes rained about the sub. The second barrage of depth charges straddled her again. She blew in half. The *O'Bannon* shook violently with the nearness of the barrage.

The searchlight went out, leaving the officers on the bridge and men on the deck temporarily blind. MacDonald blinked his dazzled eyes but could see nothing but blackness where the sub had been.

"She's under," said Simmons.

MacDonald sniffed the air.

"I think I can smell her Diesel oil," he said. Now the pungent, bitter smell, like the exhaust of a bus or truck, was unmistakable. It filled the air. MacDonald walked out to the wing of the bridge. The smell was stronger there. He looked down at the foamy side of the ship. In his mind he pictured the lake of oil swelling out over the sea. Soon bits of debris would bob to the surface. Maybe bodies. He moved back in the pilothouse.

Conn was reporting: "Unable to pick up any sound contact, Captain."

MacDonald walked to the TBS speaker.

"Jeff to Mike: I'm sure we got him."

"Mike to Jeff: Well done. Join up."

The next morning at Tulagi Captain MacDonald read a congratulatory message from Admiral Halsey to the crew:

"Congratulations for sinking the Jap. Your ingenuity in making use of all available weapons is commended."

The only one on board who refused to be enthusiastic was Pappy Rowland.

"Maybe Halsey will explain how I can put down on my books: 'One crate of potatoes. Used for bombarding a Jap submarine,'" he grumbled in the chief's quarters.

The *O'Bannon* made two more runs up the Slot before she was ordered to Noumea for a few days' rest.

In New Caledonia, baseball games were organized with the *Strong,* who accompanied the *O'Bannon.* At one of the games one of the *Strong's* officers sat next to Dr. Manchester. After the game—no one can recall who won—they walked together to the officers' club in Noumea. The air was warm but not oppressive. In the bar they sat and talked, and then, lulled by the quiet, relaxed into silence. Suddenly the *Strong's* officer said:

"You know, Doc, I have a feeling that this is our last trip."

The doctor waved him away.

"But I'm serious, Doc," the young officer insisted. "That feeling has been with me for the last few weeks. I think I'm going to die soon—and a funny thing about it, I'm not afraid."

Vaguely disturbed, Manchester launched into a description of Chief Unroe sliding for home. In a few minutes they were both roaring with laughter.

But that night back on board the *O'Bannon,* Dr. Manchester stood on deck staring out across the blacked-out town. The words of the *Strong's* officer kept coming back. Somehow he couldn't forget them.

On the return to Guadalcanal, the *Strong* sighted a Jap submarine and launched an attack. The sub dove deep, but the *Strong's* skipper, Captain Joseph Wellings, kept boiling the sea with depth charges. Finally an oil slick seeped to the surface.

"Velly solly. Jap gone," he signaled as she joined the *O'Bannon.*

Back at Tulagi again the force continued their Slot running. On the night of May 13 the *O'Bannon* was ordered to join another bombardment of Vila–Stanmore Plantation and Munda. Shipping was continuing to pour into the bases in large quantities despite the previous bombardments. It was decided to strike one of the heaviest blows of the Solomon Campaign at these spots. It was the opening phase of the ground campaign to occupy the important islands.

At the conference with the captains of the destroyers and cruisers who were to take part in the night's action, Rear Admiral Ainsworth declared:

"The only way to do it is to go in and take the fields away from the Japs."

This time the *O'Bannon* would hit Vila–Stanmore in company with the *Nicholas*, the *Taylor*, the *Strong*, and the *Chevalier*. The cruisers would be the *Helena*, the *Honolulu*, and the *Nashville*.

The Munda force consisted of one cruiser and two destroyers: The *St. Louis*, the *Jenkins* and the *Fletcher*.

The *O'Bannon* was scheduled to bombard enemy observation posts and houses where thousands of Jap troops were bivouacked.

As the force pulled out of Tulagi the sunset stained the sky a deep even red. As they passed the Russells the moon emerged from a misty cloudbank and hung in the sky like a crescent orange peel. Topside on the *O'Bannon* men cursed the moon that so plainly silhouetted the ships. Jap bombers wouldn't have much trouble tonight.

At 0030 the moon, hidden by thunderheads over Kolombangara, left a black shadow along the coastline. A fresh breeze whispered through the *O'Bannon's* rigging. Flimsy clouds sailed across the starlit sky.

The force entered the gulf. The *O'Bannon* moved in first. She seemed confident, almost arrogant. This was old stuff to her. She knew every inch of this death trap. Far across the gulf a light blinked, then vanished. Lookouts on the wings of the *O'Bannon's* bridge strained their eyes. Now the moon hung clear again.

Over the radio circuit the Black Cat pilot called:

"Testing . . . testing . . . Can you guys shoot out this damn moon?"

In the radio shack Padgett grinned. The pilot seemed a little nervous. The ships moved to the bombardment line.

Suddenly a searchlight split the darkness and began to feel about the sky, seeking the droning Black Cat. Back and forth it moved, probing each cloud with a stiff white finger. The Cat called to the force:

"I can't see . . . I can't see . . ."

79

Across the TBS Ainsworth ordered the *O'Bannon:*
"Robin to Robert: Shoot out the searchlight."
On the bridge MacDonald snapped:
"Left full rudder. . . . Director, we're going in to knock out that light. . . . Have you a solution?"
"I have, Captain."
"Commence firing."
The first salvo wiped out the Jap searchlight. The Cat immediately called back:
"Thanks, that's shooting."
The *Honolulu* opened the bombardment with all her guns. She went into continuous fire, walking her shells up and down the air strips. Jap shore batteries answered.
Fiery red balls, sailing through the air like high tennis lobs, fell about the ships. Tracers, red, green, and white, sparkled in the darkness.
The *O'Bannon,* now in her scheduled position, began her bombardment. Her shells were directed at the Kape Harbor and Lulu Lake district where thousands of Jap troops were believed camped. After the first two salvos the Cat called:
"Perfect first two . . . keep them coming . . . now you're hitting . . . I wonder what they're thinking down there . . . the Admiral can't ask for anything more."
The *O'Bannon,* feet planted deep in the sea, stood off the inlet sending round after round of screaming steel across the gulf. The *Strong* and *Chevalier* joined her. The three destroyers sent out a solid sheet of flame. Fires on the islands grew more and more intense. Once a magazine exploded and a sudden flare rose column-like in the air.
At 0114 the phantom ship was sighted again. This time "The Flying Dutchman of Kula Gulf" was reported off the *Nashville's* bow. She turned to engage but the mystery ship melted in the gloom. The Force moved down to Rice Anchorage. Fires dotted the area. The *O'Bannon's* target of Bairoko Harbor was ablaze with fire. On Ainsworth's command of "All ships join up," the force knifed its way homeward.
The Munda force could be heard bombarding their positions.

Explosions rumbled across the gulf. Outside the gulf all ships rendezvoused and headed for Tulagi.

When she returned to Tulagi, the *O'Bannon* was ordered to join a convoy of Liberty ships from New Caledonia to Guadalcanal. There was no rest at Noumea when she arrived. In a few hours she was steaming out to sea, hovering about the lumbering ships, nipping at their heels like a sheep dog tending the flock.

June 16 dawned like any other day, bright and hot—with the usual fringe of mist enshrouding the mountains of Guadalcanal. Before nightfall this day was to go down in history as "Falling Leaf Day," the day on which the Japanese Air Force suffered one of its greatest defeats.

The *O'Bannon* had taken her position off Koli Point, screening the unloading ships, when word was received of the approaching sky armada. As Captain MacDonald was sipping a second cup of coffee, Chief Padgett reported from the radio shack:

"Enemy planes headed this way. Force of 160 planes reported, Captain."

MacDonald jumped up, spilling the half-emptied cup.

"We have information air attack," he told his ship over the loudspeaker. "All hands to battle stations."

He leaned over and pressed the general-quarters alarm. Men sleeping on deck rose groggily to their feet, rubbed their eyes and rushed to battle stations. Outside the pilothouse MacDonald could hear Bill Simmons scrambling up the director, cursing as he scraped his knee on the ladder.

The Liberty ships began to move from the beaches, anxious to reach the open sea for maneuvering room. Funnels puffed out gusts of black smoke as the ships scattered, some moving off Koli Point, others slipping into Sealark Channel.

Miles away, across at Henderson Field, a dust cloud rose as the fighters took off to meet the enemy. Planes, sun glinting on their silver bellies, came in low over Savo Island. The red ball of the Rising Sun was plainly visible.

The first group peeled out of formation and dove screaming at Tulagi Harbor. The third plane in the group dropped a bomb on an oil tanker. There was a sudden flash, followed by a pall of thick, greasy smoke that seemed to be more liquid than gaseous. The rest of the planes dove at the *Taylor*, which zigzagged like a frightened chicken. Bomb bursts threw up pillars of water that obscured her completely at times, but she was unhurt. Her decks were alive with gun flashes. One, two, and then three planes blew up into splintered wreckage.

Another group attacked the twisting, dodging *O'Bannon*.

"Pick up plane . . . Fire."

MacDonald was snapping orders about the bridge, running from one wing to the other. Once he stepped on his plastic coffee cup and smashed it flat.

The planes came in from 15,000 feet in an almost vertical dive. The *O'Bannon's* guns chattered. The lead plane, without pulling out of its dive, plunged headlong into the sea. The wing of another wrenched off with the sound of a giant twisting a limb from a green tree. The Jap wobbled, crashed. Then there was an explosion and it disappeared.

The air overhead was alive with diving planes that swarmed about the ships like angry hornets. Walls of water hid the ships from sight. One LST billowed smoke. A small tanker was aflame and settling aft.

One Jap plane skimmed the water at less than fifteen feet and attacked a PT boat. The tiny craft gallantly turned to give battle and the Jap crashed less than ten feet off her stern.

All about the sea planes were burning and smoking. Ninety-seven planes had fallen from the sky.

Total casualties on the *O'Bannon*—one coffee cup.

The following day the screening force, headed by the *O'Bannon*, shepherded its flock toward Espiritu Santo. Exhausted men went to their bunks for what they called "one uninterrupted night's sleep in months."

Lieutenant Burford, who had the deck, was watching the night turn into gray emptiness. It was 0650. The languid breeze was dying and the day's heat was beginning to clutch at the air. The ship was silent. The only sound was the muted beat of her pulse. The *O'Bannon's* bow was bedecked by a misty shawl as she cut a white gash through the sea.

Suddenly there was an explosion. Lieutenant Burford picked up his binoculars. Through them he saw a Liberty ship circling slowly in the water. Flame was pouring from her reeling forecastle. In two leaps he was across the pilothouse into the captain's emergency cabin shaking MacDonald.

"Captain, our ships are being attacked."

MacDonald fumbled for his glasses hanging on a lanyard about his neck. He reached the bridge and instantly saw the burning ships.

"Sub," he said shortly. "Sound General Quarters."

There was a second explosion. A second ship was afire. Distress signals began blinking in the gray light.

"Sound, have you a contact?"

"No contact, Captain."

"They must have come from the other side," MacDonald said. At his orders the signalman on the bridge blinked:

"Close ships."

The frightened Liberty ships moved together.

MacDonald ordered the *Radford* over the TBS:

"Pick up survivors. I will search for the sub."

The *O'Bannon* scoured the area all day but the sub had successfully made her escape. In the morning medical assistance was requested, and Captain MacDonald sent Dr. Manchester across in a whaleboat to a 1,000-ton minesweeper. He climbed aboard.

Two hundred bewildered, oil-covered men crowded the decks. Several were already dead, the physician noted. One man sat like a stone statue, large black beads slowly dropping off his chin. He never moved or spoke. His terror-filled eyes were the only thing alive in his face.

The enlisted men's messhall became an emergency hospital. The dead were sorted from the living and carried to the fantail. One large seaman carefully folded the arms of one of the dead boys and, picking up the body, tenderly carried it to the deck.

"That's his brother," someone whispered, as the grim-faced, oil-covered seaman left the messhall.

Supplies of plasma were soon exhausted. A message was flashed to the *O'Bannon*. She came alongside and fired a line. The life-saving plasma was transferred at sea.

That afternoon six of the badly burned men were buried at sea. The gray clouds had opened and rain pelted down on the silent circle of uncovered men and officers gathered on the tiny port quarterdeck. The bodies of the dead men were wrapped in canvas shrouds, each draped with a dripping American flag. The men who stared at the bodies of their friends, each hidden in anonymity by the identical coverings, were grim and unshaven, some without shoes or shirts. To look at their faces no man could read their thoughts. Six seamen gently placed the bodies on tilting boards. The skipper of the minesweeper, Captain Collins, Bible in hand, began to read. The rain-filled wind tore the words from his lips. His voice rose above the throbbing of the ship's engines, the moaning of the wind through the ship's rigging, and the pelting rain.

" 'We therefore commit these bodies to the deep to be turned into corruption, looking for the resurrection when the sea shall give up her dead and the life of the world to come.' "

The seamen tipped the boards. The canvas made a scratching sound. The dead men slid beneath the surface of the sea. Silently, the officers and crew returned to their battle stations. The tiny ship, burying her nose in the whitecaps, headed for Espiritu Santo.

All that night and part of the next day the *O'Bannon* hunted the Japanese sub. Soundman Conn refused to leave his post. Several times Padgett looked in at him.

"Want to hit the sack for awhile?"

The soundman shook his head. His shirt, dark with sweat, was pasted to his back as he kept his ears alert to the constant ping of the sound gear sending its electrical impulses through the sea. In the pilothouse MacDonald and his officers waited for a contact, listening to the drumming of the rain.

Finally MacDonald ordered the *O'Bannon* to head for Espiritu Santo. The sub had made good its escape.

After she was fueled the destroyer headed back to Tulagi. She

U.S.S. *O'Bannon*—QUEEN OF THE "TIN-CAN" FLEET

LT. COMDR. DONALD J. MACDONALD RECEIVES COMMAND OF THE U.S.S. *O'Bannon*

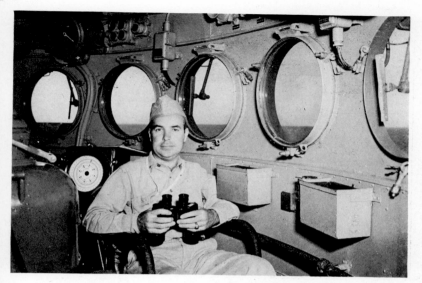

CAPTAIN MACDONALD IN THE *O'Bannon's* PILOT HOUSE

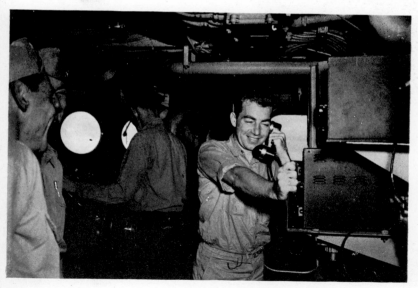

COMMUNICATIONS OFFICER CREIGH AT HIS STATION

OFFICERS' MESS

CHIEFS' QUARTERS

CREWS' QUARTERS

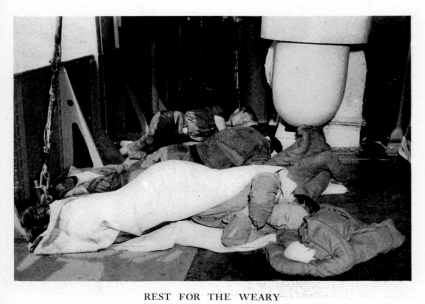

REST FOR THE WEARY

THE *O'Bannon* LEADS HER SISTERS INTO BATTLE

THE *O'Bannon* SPEEDING UP "THE SLOT"

THE "TIN-CAN" FLEET DUELS WITH A JAP BOMBER

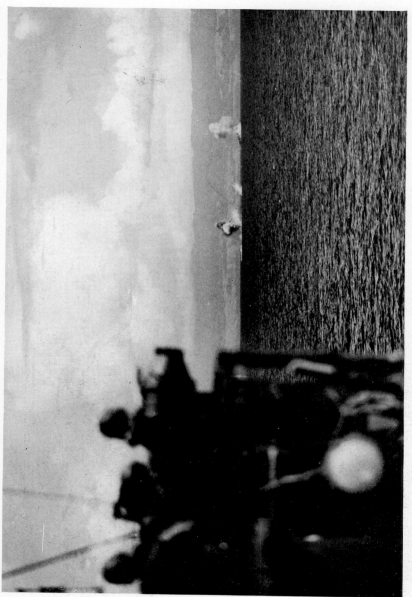

"FALLING LEAF DAY" OFF GUADALCANAL

THE *O'Bannon's* GUNS LIGHT UP THE DUSK OFF VILA-STANMORE

BLASTING MUNDA

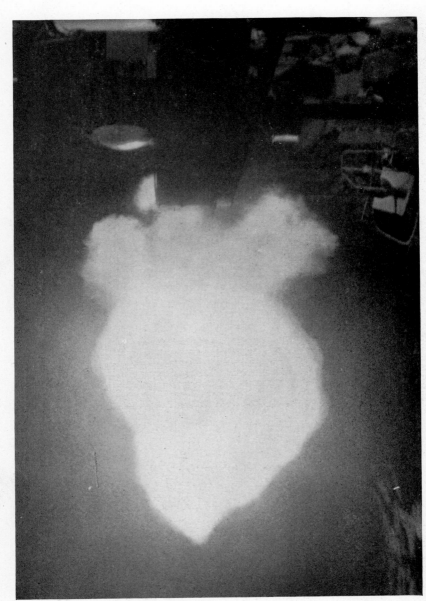

THE *O'Bannon's* GUNS RIP THE JAP FLEET IN KULA GULF

TRACERS FROM THE "TIN-CAN" FLEET WEAVE A WEB OF DEATH OFF VELLA LAVELLA

ALONE IN THE NIGHT OFF VELLA LAVELLA, THE *O'Bannon* SLUGS IT OUT WITH A JAP TASK FORCE

THE *Helena*, GUNS STILL ROARING, SINKS BENEATH THE WATERS OF KULA GULF

COMMANDER DONALD J. MACDONALD, U.S.N.

Skipper of the *O'Bannon*, Whose Seamanship and Daring Made
Him the Most Decorated Officer in the United States Navy

made another trip up the Slot and the next morning a message was handed to MacDonald. He read it and handed it to Lieutenant Philip. The executive officer grinned and gave it back to the Captain.

"That's the best news I've heard since the home team won the state cup, Captain," he said.

MacDonald walked over to the loudspeaker.

"All hands, this is your captain speaking. We are going on a trip for a short time. I can't tell you where it will be but I can tell you to get out your blues."

Weary boys stared, then cheered and pounded each other's backs. The whole ship seemed to come alive. There was laughter and animated conversation. Plans were made. That afternoon Watertender First Class Lewis E. Itzin, first wiping his hands on a greasy waste cloth, took out a large roll of greenbacks and handed it to Zimmerman.

"There's 700 dollars here, Zip, for the kids. They deserve it."

The chief was puzzled.

"What will we do with it, Itzin?"

The fireman bellowed.

"Do with it? What the hell do you think I want done with it? Hire a house and stock it with whisky, liquor, music, and laughter and a good time. Chicken and turkey, without a G. Q. alarm . . ."

He threw up his hands and walked away. Zimmerman, grinning, put the money in his locker.

That night Zimmerman and Unroe summoned their crews together.

"All of us will go on liberty very soon. It will probably take us a couple of days to get there, and it takes four days to clean a boiler. If you clean the boilers now we'll relieve a watch for some other guy to help you work and we'll have that much done. It's either do it now or when we hit port."

The next day squads of men crept into the belly of the first of the giant boilers and began the tedious job of cleaning. The men refused to waste even the few minutes it took them to climb to the crew's quarters, forward. Instead, they lay on the fireroom floor in their clothes to sleep for a few hours until their turn came again. When Pappy Rowland heard what was going on he immediately ordered trays of sandwiches and pots of coffee sent down.

Five days later the *O'Bannon* eased herself into the dock at Sydney, Australia. Several girls were passing.

"Gee, a dame," one boy yelled. One of the girls looked up. She began waving her arms.

"What the hell do you know," one of the signalmen said. "She's using semaphore. She says, 'Welcome to Australia.'"

On the bridge MacDonald told Lieutenant Philip:

"Take over, George. Give the men as much shore leave as possible. Let them have all the fun they want. We don't know when we'll come back."

Lines were cast over, and the *O'Bannon* lay quiet at her berth. The men began to troop ashore—their first shore leave since they left Bosten ten months before.

One of the first things Zimmerman did when he reached shore was to buy a new chief petty officer's uniform. After being fitted, he took it to his hotel and tried it on before a mirror. It was perfect. The phone rang. One of the chiefs wanted to know when he was coming down. Zimmerman promised it would be only a few minutes. He gave his hat a tap, brushed a few pieces of lint from a sleeve, and walked to the door. He turned to look at the bed. Cool, with crisp, clean sheets.

"The hell with it," he murmured and walking over to the bed, climbed in—uniform and all. He slept like a dead man for a day and a night.

Itzin's money was put to use the third day the *O'Bannon* was in port. Under the expert direction of Unroe and Zimmerman, caseloads of champagne, Burgundy, and Scotch; beer; mountains of sandwiches, and pastries were unloaded and hauled up to a large rented apartment.

The firemen and watertenders were assembled.

"This is yours," they were told, "with the best wishes of that ugly-faced baboon, Itzin."

The *O'Bannon* stayed for a little more than a week. A few

hours before she pulled out Lieutenant Philip told Captain Mac-Donald:

"Captain, Seaman Second Class Robert Whisler has a young puppy and he wants permission to keep it."

"Bring him up here, George," MacDonald said.

The young sailor climbed to the bridge carrying a tiny fox terrier.

"It's pedigreed, Captain," he said.

"Never mind the pedigree, son—has it been housebroken?" the Captain asked.

Whisler scratched his head.

"Gosh, sir," he replied, "I don't know. All I know is her name is Peggy."

MacDonald gave his permission.

"On one condition," he pointed out. "If she doesn't know her manners, you'll do the dirty work. Is that agreed?"

Grinning, the boy nodded.

Peggy sailed with the *O'Bannon* that night back to war. A special box was kept for her in the forward boatswain locker, and she was given the special rating of K-9. For the first week she lived in a dog's dream world. Peggy always ate her noon and evening meals at the same time absorbing affection from a half-dozen different admirers, both officers and enlisted men. One of the men ripped apart a kapok life jacket and remade it to fit Peggy's streamlined figure. Her favorite companion was Dr. Manchester. It was a common sight to see Peggy, sometimes just barely able to wobble after a siege of seasickness or overeating, hurrying after the fast-moving doctor. Peggy was his only fracture case. One day she fell off the torpedo deck as the *O'Bannon* was coming into Espiritu Santo and broke her leg. Peggy was sent over to the destroyer tender *Dixie's* sick bay with an official request for an X-ray. She received the attention of an admiral.

A lieutenant from Henderson Field gallantly postponed his own X-ray while hers was taken. The roentgenologist's official report was typed up and taken over to Dr. Manchester, who administered treatment.

When Peggy forgot her manners the crew would chorus,

"Whisler, lay up on the quarterdeck. Peggy forgot," until Peggy's master hustled up with a shovel.

The *O'Bannon* was a different ship when she steamed back to Tulagi Harbor. Men and officers still longed for home, but the bitter sense of hopelessness had been replaced by a feeling of optimism and renewed fighting spirit.

The war was rapidly moving north. The anchorages about Tulagi and Guadalcanal were starting to lose the tenseness of war. The *O'Bannon* was allowed movies which were shown each night on the forecastle. Washing Machine Charlie still droned overhead, and the ships went to General Quarters at Condition Red, but afterward they returned to finish the movies.

Ensign "Slim Jim" Garten, the assistant gunnery officer, was the movie officer. He daily promised a good "leg show," but inevitably dozens of cowboys with six-shooters blazing would race across the screen.

"Hollywood crossed me again," he would answer all complaints.

8 BATTLE OF KOLOMBANGARA

THE SKIPPER OF any destroyer has a cross to bear, for his ship is a temperamental female with a mind of her own. At the slightest provocation she may refuse to answer her rudder—with orders snapping up and down the flagship's hoist—or she may have the habit of becoming exuberant at the sight of her squat, ugly sister, the fueling ship, and unless watched like a hawk throw her fantail into the wind.

But on the *O'Bannon*, Captain MacDonald had Rivers and Lewis. Rivers—Rudolph Rivers, Officer's Cook Third Class. Lewis—Olander K. Lewis, Officer's Mess Steward.

Lewis' main trouble was shoes, while Rivers just didn't give a hoot about Navy detail.

The few requests that Captain MacDonald made were simple. A hint to Rivers for some cherry pie always worked, but when asked to lay out a clean change of uniform for Admiral Ainsworth's conference, that was when Rivers failed. He would lay out everything except the socks; another time the shirt. In the wardroom MacDonald would stiffly tell his grinning officers:

"By God, that's the last straw. I'm going to transfer him in the morning." But he never did.

And then Lewis, who insisted the Navy couldn't dig up shoes that fit his feet, would shuffle in. Every shoe he wore had the top cut away. White-coated, an eternal grin on his chocolate-brown face, he would move about the room, his shoes clicking like castanets as he served the officers, until Captain MacDonald —still smoldering about the forgotten socks—would bellow:

"Dammit Lewis, if you don't get shoes that fit your feet I'll send you ashore in the morning."

Lewis would nod seriously and tiptoe out to borrow a shipmate's shoes.

A few days later the castanets would start clicking again, and Captain MacDonald would groan and promise himself that he would dictate a note that very day to Washington to the Navy's supply department to canvass the states for shoes to fit his officer's mess steward.

But "Captain Mac" was Rivers' special charge. He had a deep pleasant voice, and in the messmen's quarters the crew listened to even his most banal stories. His favorite topic was the likes and dislikes of Captain MacDonald.

"For breakfast," he would say, "that man drinks nothing but coffee. One, two, three, four, or even five cups. Damn, how that man likes coffee. Maybe sometimes, he takes a piece of toast. But when he's got troubles he just sits there talking to Mistuh Philip, sipping away at that old coffee."

No one on the *O'Bannon* watched their skipper with as much affection as did Rivers. After long weary nights of bombarding or fighting off Jap air attacks while Slot running, a plate of sandwiches and a mug of hot coffee would magically appear at MacDonald's elbow, and the Captain would mentally forgive Rivers' sins of forgetfulness.

But to the men of the *O'Bannon*, Rivers was a grim prophet.

As each day wore on to the late afternoon the crew would follow his every movement.

Men chipping rust spots on a bulkhead would watch him as he shuffled down the deck. Their eyes searched eagerly for one thing—the large black thermos bottle belonging to Captain MacDonald. If he carried it they would groan to themselves. By now that innocent-appearing coffee container had become a grim symbol of MacDonald never leaving his bridge as they steamed up the Slot; tense hours of standing at battle stations, bombardments, perhaps meeting the enemy with roaring guns and ships exploding like powder factories. To the men's over-alertness for any possible variation of the *O'Bannon's* fate, the simple picture of a slow-moving Negro boy holding a black thermos bottle was enough to create enormous conjectures and black forebodings. Once a seaman sprawled on the weather deck said:

"Oh nuts, maybe the old man just wants a drink of iced tea." But the men around turned on him as if he had cursed the *O'Bannon* herself. Rivers and the black thermos bottle were an integral part of the ship's life. The sight of them was as much a part of the *O'Bannon's* preparation for going into battle as was the urgent call of General Quarters.

In the beginning Rivers was ready to tell anyone who stopped him: "Looks like a little business tonight, boy, Captain asking for his thermos filled with coffee." But as the days went on he came to recognize it as a mysterious ritual, and when stopped he would smile and pass without speaking.

And so on the afternoon of July 4 Rivers entered the galley. Even Pappy Rowland stopped to watch him. He picked up the coffeepot—filled with coffee every hour of the day or night—and carefully filled the Captain's thermos. He scowled as his brown fingers firmly screwed on the top. Topside he walked along the deck and climbed to the pilothouse. Word passed swiftly around the ship. It actually seemed to seep through the bulkheads. In a few minutes firemen below decks knew that to-night the *O'Bannon* was "going somewhere."

There was nothing on which to base the rumor. But to the men on the *O'Bannon* it was truth—as much truth as if Executive Officer Philip had touched each man and whispered in his ear: "We are going into the darkness again tonight. I don't know what will happen but tomorrow we all may be dead."

They pulled out at sunset, and as they steamed into the gathering darkness Captain MacDonald told his men what lay in store for them. It was another bombardment. The New Georgia campaign had begun. This time a landing was to take place on Rice Anchorage to prevent Munda from receiving reinforcements from Kolombangara. Vila–Stanmore, Bairoko Harbor, and Enogai Inlet were to be blasted. The force that night consisted

91

of the cruisers *Honolulu, Helena, St. Louis,* and Tulagi's eternal tin-can fleet, the *O'Bannon, Nicholas, Strong,* and *Chevalier.*

"This is an important mission tonight, men," Captain Mac-Donald concluded over the ship's loudspeaker, "and we must be prepared for anything. I know I can rely on you as I have done in the past. That is all."

The night was pitch-black. The moon had gone down behind Kolombangara's mountain as they entered Kula Gulf. A stiff breeze sprang up, and the water was soon dotted with white caps. As they swung into bombardment line Jap searchlights began searching the sky for Black Cat planes overhead.

The *O'Bannon* and the *Chevalier* opened the bombardment. Torrents of steel fell on the island. The searchlight went out. The sky became alive with a tracery of glowing shells—the fifteen-shell pattern of the cruisers' salvo fire, the lesser five-shell pattern of the destroyers' guns.

Firing by the Jap shore batteries was heavy. The entire gulf glowed with a weird light as the waters played with the flashes they caught from the guns.

In the pilothouse over the TBS Rear Admiral Ainsworth reported the *Strong* was missing. He asked the *Chevalier:*

"Princess to Queen: Where is Mary? I can't find her."

Just then MacDonald picked up the *Strong* through his glasses. A shower of flares exploded about her. A blinker light flashed. She had been hit and was sinking fast.

Over the TBS MacDonald informed Ainsworth:

"King to Princess: Mary is dead in the water on my starboard side. Flares overhead and about her. Shall I help?"

"Princess to King: Assist Mary. Take Queen."

"Left full rudder . . . all ahead full . . ." MacDonald brought the *O'Bannon* about in a full circle and started back into the pitch-black gulf. The *Chevalier,* on her port hand, signaled as they drew close.

"Queen to King: I will take off the survivors. You take care of shore batteries."

Flares burst high in the blackness and drifted slowly about the

Strong's rigging. She was dying fast. Now she lay on her starboard side pillowing herself against the swells. She stayed there, lifeless in her lethargy.

Through his glasses MacDonald caught the scurrying figures of the crew abandoning their ship. Against the background of the flares they looked like walking flames. The *Chevalier* moved closer to the *Strong*. Shore batteries suddenly began blazing away at the three ships. Their fire was directed at the *Strong* and the *Chevalier*. Shells began falling about them, ready, as the Jap gunners got the exact range, to stamp on them. MacDonald made a quick decision. He would go between the shore batteries and the *Chevalier* and the dying *Strong*.

"Right 15 . . . steady on nine-oh . . ."

"Steady on nine-oh, sir."

The *O'Bannon* moved closer to the batteries disgorging their reddish balls of fire. One splashed off her bow. The column of water rose higher than the bridge.

On the flying bridge, Ensign H. P. Burford, who had been made secondary gunnery officer when Lieutenant Ditto was transferred after the last bombardment, heard a faint sighing. It grew louder and louder until it became a scream overhead. Another and another followed. The Jap gunners were throwing all they had at the *O'Bannon*. Now MacDonald ordered:

"All engines . . . Stop!"

The *O'Bannon* slowed to a walk, paused, then stopped dead in the water. The shoreline blinked with gun blasts. Pillars of water rose on all sides of the ship. Once a "daisy cutter" exploded off her port and fragments of shrieking steel rained about the superstructure.

When the paralyzing order was given, men in the fireroom and engine rooms looked at each other in amazement. They seemed like a group of men beset by many things and then suddenly faced with a heavy and unexpected burden. The trips up the Slot had been numerous during the last few months. The fear that twisted their stomachs into tight knots, that lay about their minds like an evil shroud, was there every night. If the

O'Bannon had been sunk by planes or by a task force her men would have accepted it coldly; factually. But this was something different. They waited.

Zimmerman, who had the phones, asked young Finley, the smoke watch on the bridge:

"What's doing, kid?"

Up to now the boy's voice had been calmly describing the bombardment. When the order to cut the engines came he was silent. Suddenly his voice screamed in Zimmerman's ear. The chief winced and held one earphone away from his head. The voice echoed tinnily through the room above the panting of the resting fireboxes.

"We're dead in the water . . . Holy God, we're going right into those shore guns . . . they're coming fast . . . Zip . . . oh, Zip . . . they're going right overhead . . . right through the rigging . . . I can see the splashes all about us . . . we're going to get it sure . . . Jesus!"

He stopped. The Holy Name hung in the air. The men in the room could feel the concussion of the shells as they churned the sea about the ship. Unroe, huge, naked to the waist, his sweat-drenched body glistening in the dim light, stared at Zimmerman who licked dry lips. Pop Popino, black hair plastered against his forehead, chewed on the stub of a pencil he used to mark the cardboard scoreboard when the *O'Bannon* launched her torpedoes; Gregory kept rolling a greasy cloth between the palms of his hands. All eyes watched the earphones. Once Itzin, whose brother was on the *Nicholas*, said,

"Ask 'em how the Nick is," but nobody answered. The long seconds ticked by. Several times concussions slammed along the steel sides of the ships. Then Unroe said:

"Maybe he's hit by shrapnel, Zip."

Zimmerman nodded and opened his mouth to ask the question, but the tinny voice began shouting:

"The *Strong* is going down . . . the *Chevalier* is standing by to take 'em. We're between them and the beach . . . Flares are falling all around the *Strong* . . . They're firing at her now . . . God, they hit her on Number One mount. Those Jap bastards are getting closer . . . Here we go, the old man told Simmons to open fire . . ."

The *O'Bannon* had drifted to less than 200 yards off the *Strong* and the *Chevalier*. She was in direct line of the blazing shore batteries and less than 4,000 yards off the beach.

"Bill, get on those gun flashes and commence firing."

MacDonald was surprised his voice sounded so calm and even. A large white-and-green flare floated midships off the *O'Bannon*, bobbing in the swells. On the flying bridge Ensign Burford thought:

"Just like the park at home on July Fourth night." Then he added with a surprised start: "Hell, this is July Fourth."

In the director Simmons was listening to Chief Fire Controlman Bess chanting the range. He pressed a buzzer. Red lights flashed in the gun mounts. The snouts of the guns lifted, moved cautiously, felt the darkness for the right level. At Simmons' touch on the firing button they spoke. Bodies jerked with the recoil in the fireroom. The guns fired rapidly for a few minutes, then stopped. Finley's voice came pouring out of the phones, words tumbling over each other.

". . . Our guns are dead . . . our guns are dead . . ."

A shell from the Jap batteries exploded off the *O'Bannon's* side. The concussion was heavier. Lights flickered. Zimmerman felt a chill closing about his heart. The guns were out, their breeches locked with the heat of the fierce bombardment. But then one began to go off in rapid fire. Again and again it barked. Finley was saying:

"They got Number One gun going." Someone near Zimmerman said: "Thank God."

In the dimness of that mount Gunner's Mate Miller was kneeling beside the breech. In his fist he held a small leather mallet. He slid his hand under and hit the breech. It closed. The gun fired. The empty shell chattered out of the mount onto the deck. The loader standing beside him dropped another one. Miller hit the breech. It fired again. As fast as the shells and powder tins slid up the hoist from Pappy Rowland's handling room they were fed to the gun. It was like a voracious iron mouth. After the first

95

several shells were fired, Miller found there was no longer any feeling in his hand, but he kept on whacking the breech and the gun went on firing.

Through his glasses MacDonald saw the *Strong* swing around in a radical circle and charge toward the *Chevalier*. He could picture the hurried confusion on the bridge as orders were shouted and men held fast at the cry: "Stand by for collision." He saw the *Strong* crash into the *Chevalier's* portside as a burst of flares exploded, lighting the sky brilliantly. The black waters of the gulf glowed with patches of silver. Another shell from the shore exploded on the *Strong*. A gun mount flew in the air. The ships were locked together. The *Chevalier* tried to shoot a hawser across the sinking ship, but the *Strong's* stern was already under. There wasn't any use.

The *O'Bannon's* one gun was still firing. Flashes on the island showed hits were scored. Moving to the TBS MacDonald asked the *Chevalier:*

"King to Queen: Have you got them off?"

"Queen to King: Not yet. Shore fire heavy. Can't maneuver. Keep clear. Might ram you . . . gyrocompass out. Sound gear gone. Taking water forward."

The shore batteries seemed to sense the desperate situation out there in the blackness. They opened with renewed fury, and the shore became alive with orange flashes. Salvos splashed about the *O'Bannon's* bow and sides. Steel moaned through the air about her bridge. Seaman Louis Cianca at his 20-mm.-gun station thought of the day Boatswain McGrath asked him, "Are you sure you want that job, Cianca?", and he groaned at the memory.

The *Chevalier* broke in:

"Queen to King: She's dying fast. My bulkheads holding. I have officers and men. I am clearing out. Please lead me."

Now, at 0122, the *Chevalier* backed away from the *Strong*. In the harsh light they could see her in a last surge of strength lift herself out of the sea, her death struggles turning the water white with acres of hissing, bubbling foam. Then she plunged down, stern first, and vanished.

The *Strong* was dead.

The *Chevalier* reported over TBS: "Mary died at 0126."

Someone on the *O'Bannon's* bridge said: "She died like a lady." That was Mitchell, MacDonald thought, he knows how to describe things. He turned to the quartermaster. "All ahead full."

The *O'Bannon* started to move away when a terrible roar filled the air. The grave of the *Strong* was erupting into a column of water that grew high and higher. The *O'Bannon* leapt forward, shuddered, but kept on her course.

Down in the fireroom Zimmerman shouted: "What was that . . . what was it?"

Finley called back: "The *Strong's* depth charges went off."

On the bridge MacDonald and his officers were flung hard against the bulkhead of the pilothouse. Floating flares showed them the inferno of exploding, erupting water.

"My God, nobody could live in that," someone cried.

Reports flowed in from repair parties. "No damage in engine rooms, firerooms." Hugging her sister destroyer, who moved with a wounded, nervous gait, the *O'Bannon* passed out of the gulf. Across the water lights blinked. It was the landing force coming into Rice Anchorage.

But the Japs weren't finished with the *O'Bannon* yet. Shore batteries on Kolombangara and Enogai Inlet opened up. Shells and flares exploded about her. But her one gun answered shell for shell. On the third round the battery was silenced.

Dr. Manchester, inspecting the ship to make sure nobody had been injured by flying fragments, went into the wardroom and found Lewis sitting in a chair. The boy looked up:

"Doctuh Manchester, when I'se a little boy mah dad tole me to always run away from trouble, but now we jes keep running into mo' and mo'."

"The thing to do is to pray, Lewis," Manchester said gravely.

"Yes, suh, Doctor, I done prayed," he said. "I'se prayed for you, I'se prayed for the ship, I'se prayed for all the officers, I'se prayed for the men, and I'se prayed for me. Now I'se jes gottuh go back to the States for mo' prayers."

At daybreak the *O'Bannon* and the *Chevalier* headed back to Tulagi. On deck Chief Gunner's Mate Spracklin was growling at Miller, whom he had had to drag out of Number One gun mount:

"I didn't want you to kill yourself. What the hell do you want to be—a hero?"

Miller grinned ruefully at his hand. It was raw and torn with deep gashes, and swollen three times its size.

"Aw, the hell with it," he said.

On the bridge MacDonald tipped the thermos and sipped Rivers' hot coffee.

9 KULA GULF

IT WAS LATE the next afternoon. Captain MacDonald was sitting on the small wooden bench one of the carpenter's mates had made for him on the port bridge wing. Dinner had been cleared, and MacDonald reminded himself to compliment Rowland on the tasty cherry pie. It had been a blistering day. Since the battle of Kolombangara the night before, the *O'Bannon* and the other ships of the force had been steaming steadily toward Tulagi Anchorage. Most of the crew, except those on watch, were sleeping on deck, hugging the shadows of the torpedo tubes, the gun mounts, or the rafts on the weather deck.

Below him on the forecastle one of the machinist's mates, a tall, husky boy by the name of Smith, was doing his daily exercises. Captain MacDonald never failed to watch him. By now he knew every move. First the blanket stretched neatly across the deck. Then the small wooden box opened, the two dumbbells taken out. The few test motions and then the exercises—up . . . down . . . one . . . two . . . three . . . From his seat, Captain MacDonald could see the play of muscles beneath the tanned skin of the boy's back, and the set, serious expression on his face.

Fifteen minutes and it was finished. The dumbbells back in the box, the blanket neatly folded, and Smith walking back to the showers. After mentally following the exercises with Smith, Captain MacDonald would find himself bathed in perspiration.

"Wonderful for the condition, George," he told his executive officer, "and I don't have to do any work. Smith does it all."

99

Suddenly the TBS, which had been silent all afternoon except for routine orders, barked with life.

"Princess to TF: Stand by to execute turn . . . Execute turn."

Captain MacDonald leaped to his feet.

"Right full rudder," he snapped to Quartermaster Gotschall, who spun the helm, heeling the *O'Bannon* about in a sharp turn.

Back on the wings of the bridge he could see the line of ships making a perfect U turn, heading back up the Slot.

"God," he thought, "we can't be going back now . . ."

The TBS answered him.

"Princess to TF: We must proceed up the Slot at once. An enemy task force has been sighted. We will meet them off Kolombangara tonight. Kitty (*Chevalier*) will proceed to base with survivors."

Ensign Creigh, who was officer of the deck, came over to stand at Captain MacDonald's elbow.

"We're going back up there, Captain?" he asked.

"I'm afraid so, John," MacDonald answered. "Probably won't meet a thing." He could sense the false cheerfulness in his voice. In the silence that followed, thoughts spun through his mind.

"Ammunition low. Only enough for twenty minutes of concerted fire. Men dead tired. We've all been alerted for six days now . . ."

He turned to Creigh, still searching the Captain's face for a possible clue to what he might expect for the night.

"Pass the word, John, to the mess officer, and have him put the wardroom dinner and the crew's mess up an hour. You might tell Rowland to try and get up something special for the men."

"Aye, aye, Captain," Creigh said, and turned and walked out of the pilothouse. Lieutenant Philip, who had been awakened by the swift turn of the ship, appeared.

"We're going back, George," MacDonald said.

The executive officer nodded. "General Quarters same time, Captain?" he asked. The Captain turned around.

"Same time, George. God, it seems as if it sounded only a few hours ago."

The sun, which had scorched the ships all day, was now sinking in a blood-red bed of clouds. For a few minutes the *O'Bannon* moved through soft golden light.

Then the air became blue; in a few minutes darkness fell, and a full moon came out to lay a path of troubled silver across the path of the moving ships, illuminating even the darkest corners.

"Beautiful, isn't it?" MacDonald murmured. Lieutenant Philip, rapidly blinking his eyes to try to rid them of the weariness that threatened to close them at any second, nodded. Through the moon-filled port he could see the *O'Bannon's* sister ships, in perfect, even line. His sailor's eye caught the eagerness of their bows as they nudged the sea, spray flying like diamond chips. They were riding hard. Under his feet the *O'Bannon's* steel body quivered. Twenty-seven knots, he estimated. He turned to MacDonald, who was smothering a yawn and rubbing a hand across his cheek.

Troubled by the weary eyes smudged by dark hollows, he asked:

"Why don't you get some rest for the next hour or two, Captain?"

MacDonald hesitated, then said:

"Maybe I will, George. I'll be in the emergency cabin. Call me on any order from the flagship."

He walked across the pilothouse to the tiny space bulkheaded from the rest of the bridge. It was scarcely bigger than a piano crate. The bulkheads were painted a dull gray color. The only furniture was a tiny desk, a straight-backed chair, and his bunk. Ignoring the chair, he sat on the bunk and slipped off his shoes. Hands behind his head he stretched out. His eyes wandered about in the gloom of the room until they caught the outlines of a picture frame on his desk. The details of that picture were as familiar to him as his own hands. Even in the darkness he thought he could make out the slightly tilted head, the shy smile, and the tawny-colored hair that spilled about her shoulders.

Unconsciously he touched his left breast pocket and could feel the outline of the small St. Christopher's medal she had given him the night the *O'Bannon* left Boston. He closed his eyes and he could see her face.

It was again that night, and she was saying: "I'll be waiting, Donald."

As he thought about it now his reply had been too simple. He wondered why he hadn't said something long and full of emotion like men do when they go to war in Hollywood. But no, all he had said was, "Thank you, Cecilia."

Now, through the brightly lit corners of his mind other scenes arose. It was London, and he was sitting in that small, quiet restaurant studying the menu. The dumpy little waiter—who always insisted on calling him "Major"—was impatiently tapping his pencil against his pad. MacDonald remembered how he had been debating ordering the boiled beef when the crash came. It was like a slow-motion picture. People jumped up; a woman screamed and a man picked up his derby and placed it carefully on his head. From a deep gash in the wall across the room dirty brown smoke curled from an unexploded bomb. He walked over to the wall. Afterward he never could explain why. In his hand he still carried the menu. He stared at the wisps of smoke. Even now he could taste the acrid bitterness. Then, carefully placing the menu on a table, he followed the patrons crowding from the restaurant. Outside he watched the searchlights probing the sky for the raider, while antiaircraft guns coughed up their flak. Later that night, when the full blitz resumed, a second bomb exploded the first, ripping the restaurant and the entire block to shattered rubble. . . . Everything seemed so long ago. His eyes began to close. He could feel his clothes sticking to his body in the cabin's humid quiet. He wondered if they would get it tonight. He wondered where the Japs were getting all their ships. He tried to remember the name of that tall, lanky Black Cat pilot with the handlebar mustache who guided their shots on the first Munda bombardment. He wondered. . . .

The quivering of the ship caressed him. He slept.

As the *O'Bannon's* engines throbbed harder, men who were asleep on deck were awakened by shipmates.

"But we've just come back . . . Christ they can't send us back . . ." they said incredulously.

". . . What the hell are we going to shoot, peanuts?" they asked and then cursed long and savagely.

In the galley, Pappy had received MacDonald's order.

"Okay," he said, "I'll give the kids a dinner. I'll give them a turkey dinner, that's what I'll do. They'll be shark bait tomorrow anyway."

As the *O'Bannon* cut through the moonlight, Lieutenant Philip found Rivers at his elbow.

"You can bring up Captain MacDonald's thermos of coffee as usual, Rivers," he told the colored boy.

"We going to see any action tonight, Mr. Philip?"

The executive officer nodded, and Rivers sighed and tucked the thermos under his arm and shuffled out of the pilothouse.

Halfway up the Slot, nature favored the force. As quickly as it had appeared, the moon hid itself behind a bank of black thunderheads. The night became pitch-black. Visibility was less than a mile. The Captain had been called by Lieutenant Philip and now sat in his armchair. Torpedo Officer Mitchell, standing on the portwing of the bridge, remembered a story he once read. It was about a famous murderer who was to die that night in Sing-Sing's death house. One part still stuck in Mitchell's mind. It had started off—

". . . And when the head keeper brought him word that the Governor had refused his attorney's appeal on grounds that new evidence had been uncovered, he was reported as saying:

" 'Well I guess I have nothing to do now except wait.' "

"So this is the way it feels," Mitchell thought. "Nothing to do except wait."

At 2000 two more ships, the destroyers *Jenkins* and *Radford*, joined the force. They took their places screening the column. It was then that Ainsworth announced over the TBS:

"Princess to TF: If enemy units are not contacted by 0145 we will retire."

At 2300 MacDonald ordered General Quarters sounded. Minutes, then hours ticked by. As the time drew near the quarter-master called:

"It is 0140 and no signal. All is quiet."

"Five more minutes, Captain," Philip said softly. There was silence. Gotschall said, "0141 and no signal."

At 0142 the TBS ordered:

"Princess to TF: Take battle formation."

MacDonald turned to Quartermaster Gotschall. "Hard right rudder," he ordered. Behind her the three cruisers and two other destroyers moved into position. Now a cruiser reported over TBS:

"Margie to Princess: Enemy ships sighted. Single line off Kolombangara." There were a few seconds of silence and again she said:

"Margie to Princess: More enemy ships sighted. Second group. Five destroyers, heavy cruisers."

The Japanese force was sailing down close to the Kolomban-gara coastline. Their ships were approaching Visu Visu Point, New Georgia, northeast of the mouth of Kula Gulf, and were coming through the narrow bottleneck of the gulf. They prob-ably had entered it by way of Blackett Strait, which separates Kolombangara's southern shore from Arundel Island. The Jap force was now identified as two light cruisers, shielded by three destroyers in front of two more heavy cruisers. They were all in standard formation.

Ainsworth's force was now running west on a course which was taking him past Kolombangara's north shore. As the Jap ships came up past Waugh Rock off Kolombangara's densely wooded shoulder hill, Ainsworth executed—in the blackness—the greatest of all naval maneuvers.

The *O'Bannon* and her sister ships crossed the Japs' "T."

As the Jap column came north to begin its westward course around Kolombangara Island, Ainsworth's ships, still on their westward course, moved in formation across the head of the Jap column—not only crossing the Japs' "T," but pinning them against the solid wall of the shore. It was then the lookout re-ported:

"Contact."

MacDonald asked over the TBS:

"King to Princess: We have contact. May we have permission to open fire?"

"Princess to King: Commence firing."

In the director, Lieutenant Simmons heard MacDonald's voice:

"Bill, have you targets?"

His answer was steady. "Aye, aye, sir."

"Fire."

The *O'Bannon's* guns thundered instantly. Salvos moaned across the sky. The *Nicholas* joined her off her starboard side, and the guns of both sisters roared with fury.

The Jap column broke in confusion. Some ships were turning back to Bougainville. One ship was dead in the water, sinking fast. Another, hit by the *O'Bannon's* first salvo, moved to the beach.

Ainsworth ordered his ships to close for the attack:

"Attack."

As they swung into position MacDonald caught a large four-stack cruiser rushing down off his bow, churning the swells into foam.

"Stand by to get that big one, Mitch," he ordered. Bess was already chanting the bearing and range. The clear voice of the torpedo officer called:

"Torpedo tubes stand by . . . fire one . . . fire two . . ."

There was a loud swish in the fireroom. "Pop" reached up to mark his scoreboard as the sulphur smell was sucked in by the lips of the blowers.

Zimmerman pushed the earphones over his head and asked Finley on the smoke watch:

"What have we got up there, kid?"

The boy's voice came back:

"There's a big guy coming down at us, Zip. . . . We just got an order to go in. . . . Well, fellows, here we go again . . . Hold your hats gang . . ."

The *O'Bannon* was making all the speed she could muster as

she went in for the torpedo run. Her blowers were at a shrill pitch and her fantail flat in the sea. Once or twice she hit large swells, and green water covered her forecastle and ran down the scuppers.

Zimmerman held the earphones away from his head as Finley's voice rose with excitement.

"We hit that big one square. She's blazing like hell. The *Helena* is throwing everything she's got at them. . . . One bastard is burning like a powder factory . . ."

"How's the Nick?" Zimmerman interrupted.

"Tell Itzin she's throwing up plenty of fire," Finley shouted back. The chief turned around and looked questioningly at Itzin, who grinned and bobbed his head up and down like a delighted satyr.

On the *O'Bannon's* starboard hand the *Helena* was showering the Jap ships with continuous fire. Two more ships exploded and one lay burning fiercely in a sea of flaming oil. The *O'Bannon* and the *Jenkins* joined the *Helena's* firings. The flash and roar of the guns shook the night. A great flaming arc of shells coursed into the enemy's column. Another ship blew up and the flaming arc changed its bearing. Just as quickly another Jap ship was hit, the flames momentarily lighting up its superstructure and rigging. The night was turned into a hellish pageant of screaming shells, brilliant red-and-white tracer arcs, and blinding blasts from salvo fire. The *Helena* had gone into continuous fire. She was completely outlined by her own gun blasts. Shell fire ripped away a Jap's superstructure and clawed at the body until it exploded in a sheet of flame, hundreds of feet in the air. The Jap cruiser hit by the *O'Bannon* moved about like a huge sea animal with broken hindquarters. MacDonald turned to Mitchell.

"Give her a couple more." He heard Mitchell cry:

"Stand by torpedo tubes . . . Fire four . . . five . . . six . . ."

The crippled Jap caught all three fish. The flash was electric white. Three explosions followed. The first was a pure white sheet of fire that shot up 200 feet in the air; the second towered above the first; the last enveloped the entire ship in a flaming shroud. In less than a minute darkness set over the spot where she sank.

The TBS ordered:

"Princess to TF: We will make a simultaneous turn and get the others on the reserve course."

All ships swung about in a 180-degree turn, which brought them back to their original course but on the opposite heading. The column had again succeeded in crossing the Japs' "T"— broadsides across bows, ready to blast the Japs to bits of wreckage.

The *Helena* continued her fire. Another Japanese cruiser was hit and burned fiercely. In ten minutes the battle was over. The remaining Jap ships fled back to Bougainville. Someone reported from the wing of the bridge:

"The Japs are beaching themselves, Captain."

As the force moved together preparing to leave, Lieutenant Simmons asked in the director:

"Captain, are all our ships accounted for? I think one is missing."

MacDonald, moving over to the TBS speaker, asked:

"King to Princess: Are all ships counted?"

There was no reply. Suddenly a lookout called:

"Object on the starboard bow."

"God," MacDonald thought, "that's no Jap. They are on the other side." As the ships passed the object the *Nicholas* searchlight flickered briefly. From the bridge they could see a jagged bow of a ship, the large numerals, 50, plainly visible.

"Good God," MacDonald cried, "it's the *Helena*."

He heard something fall. Chief Yeoman Fahrbach, who through the battle had been in his niche underneath the table, dropped his flashlight. "It's the *Helena*," he echoed, "God, it can't be."

On the smoke watch Finley was shouting:

"Zip . . . Zip . . . they just picked up the *Helena* . . . she's sunk . . . I can see her bow from here . . . there's a 50

on it . . . Zip . . . Now we got a blinker from the *Nicholas*
. . . she's shooting flares . . . she's standing by . . . Christ
. . . it's the *Helena* all right . . ."

The Captain's solemn voice reached throughout the ship:

"I am sorry to inform you men that the *Helena* has been sunk.
The *Nicholas* and the *Radford* are standing by to pick up survivors. That is all."

In the fireroom a boy cried: "She can't be gone," and sat
down on a bench and wept.

Bewildered crew members stood looking at each other. The
mighty *Helena* sunk? Hell, someone was fouled up somewhere.
No Jap could sink the *Helena*. Their thought was the same, from
the messmen in their steamy handling room deep in the belly of
the ship to the stunned officers on the bridge.

After he had made the announcements to the crew Captain
MacDonald stared out through the nearest port. He fumbled for
his pipe and clenched it between his teeth. The picture of what
was happening in the blackness behind him flashed across his
mind. Men, some horribly burned, paddling about the water,
hoping and praying that someone would turn about and help
them. Jap planes overhead waiting for the rescue ships. Somewhere out there Jap ships still lurked. He said, half to himself:

"Help them and protect them, O merciful God."

Philip turned, "Did you say something, Captain?"

"I was just wishing them Godspeed, George," MacDonald
said.

The executive officer nodded:

"So was I, sir," he said softly.

It was near daybreak when the force drew near Tulagi. Captain MacDonald and his officers were still at their stations on
the bridge. There had been no sleep and little conversation since
the battle scene. The sun was just breaking through the morning mists, turning the sea from lead to gold, when the TBS
broke the silence.

"Princess to TF: We have received word that the *Radford*
and the *Nicholas* have been forced to retire because of heavy

Japanese air attacks. Several hundred men have been rescued but there are many more survivors in the water. That is all."

MacDonald, his hand lifting a cup of coffee, sat frozen, the cup a few inches from his lips. Philip, Mitchell, and the rest of the officers stared unbelievingly at the grille of the loudspeaker. Placing the cup carefully on the table, MacDonald said: "I must inform the men." He moved heavily to his feet. At the ship's loudspeaker he said slowly:

"Men, this is your captain. I have just received word from the flagship that the *Radford* and the *Nicholas* have been forced to leave the area where the *Helena* had gone down as a result of heavy air attacks. I am sorry to tell you this. I know your affection for the *Helena's* men, but the information is that there are many survivors still in the water. That is all."

His words had scarcely died away when a strange scene took place. From the wings of the bridge Signalman First Class Daniel Brown had stepped into the pilothouse. His hands were trembling, his voice strained and hoarse as he spoke:

"Captain, we must go back for them . . . We must, Captain . . . We can't leave them there . . ."

MacDonald, taken by surprise, arched his eyebrows. He started to speak, but behind him Chief Radioman Padgett was saying:

"Please, Captain, we must go back." More men crowded into the pilothouse from all parts of the ship . . . Unroe, his oil-streaked chest visible through the open shirt, Zimmerman, wiping his hands nervously down the sides of his pants, tight lines around his mouth . . . Bess from the fire control . . . and then his officers . . . Philip . . . Mitchell . . . Creigh . . . Eardley . . . all nodding their heads.

MacDonald felt a surge of pride rise in his throat. When he managed to speak his voice was deep and husky.

"You know what this means, men?"

Padgett, who was nearest the Captain, said: "I think we all know, Captain."

But MacDonald persisted. He turned to his officers. His eyes touched each one. "You know we may not come back?"

They all nodded. MacDonald hesitated, then stepped to the loudspeaker. He stared intently at it as he spoke.

"All hands, this is your captain. I have received numerous requests from your chief petty officers that we turn about and rescue the remaining *Helena* survivors. Your loyalty touches me, but the hazards of this mission make me consider that before I request permission from the admiral I would like to hear from more of you. If you are all in favor of going back I will request permission, and if I receive it we will go back. I want your petty officers to ascertain your desires and let me know as soon as they can. That is all."

Silently the CPO's filed out of the pilothouse and to their stations.

In fire control Bess asked his men: "Are you unwilling to go up?"

In one voice they answered: "You're damn right we want to go up, Chief."

In the fireroom Zimmerman and Unroe slid down the ladder and faced the boys who crowded about them. "The Captain wants to know if you're willing to go back."

Popino, his slim, sweat-drenched body glistening in the dim light, the stub of his pencil in his mouth, growled:

"Hell, they'd go for us, wouldn't they, Zip?"

Zimmerman nodded. His eyes jumped from face to face . . . the blond Conklin brothers, huge, towering above the others . . . Gregory, nonchalant . . . Itzin, his small black goatee giving him a strange Mephistophelian look . . . Fleming, grinning . . . all saying,

"Sure, Zip . . . Go ahead and tell 'em, Unroe . . . What the hell are we waiting for? . . . Let's go."

Unroe touched Zimmerman on the arm. They both climbed the ladder to the deck. The whole ship was buzzing. Sleep and rest were forgotten. Pappy Rowland was roaring at his messmen: "Damn right we'll go back."

On the bridge the CPO's trooped in and faced MacDonald. The pilothouse was crowded. Every chief and officer on the ship was represented. They all stood silent, watching their skipper. At last MacDonald said:

"What do the men say?"

Brown spoke up: "They all want to go back, Captain."

The other CPO's broke in with: "My men want to go back . . . The fireroom is ready, Captain . . . All the engineers want to go . . . My radiomen are ready . . ."

MacDonald turned to Brown:

"Brown, are you sure your men know what this means?"

The signalman replied: "Yes, sir, even if they know they might be dead tonight."

Chief Boatswain Charles Picton called out from the edge of the group:

"The deck force all realize how dangerous it is, but we're all ready."

Lieutenant Philip summed it up briefly with: "The ship is ready, Captain."

On the forecastle men who were able to do so without leaving their watch clustered in small, tight, silent groups, their eyes glued on the open ports of the pilothouse. On either side of the *O'Bannon* the ships of the formation rolled deep into the sea, shaking off sheets of water from their preening bows.

MacDonald turned to Brown. His voice was brisk:

"Send a message to the flagship: The *O'Bannon*, realizing the hazards of the mission, wishes to volunteer to return alone to rescue the *Helena* survivors."

Brown saluted and moved to the flag hoist on the wings of the bridge. In the pilothouse the men could hear the clang of the lid of the metal flagbags.

"I will notify you as soon as I receive the message," MacDonald said. The CPO's saluted, returning to their stations. The Captain slumped in his chair. Silence hung about the ship.

An hour later Brown shouted:

"Message from the flagship, sir." MacDonald jumped to the wings of the bridge. Brown was already reading:

"We appreciate your offer. We understand the emotions that prompted your request, but it cannot be done at this time."

A few minutes later MacDonald told his crew:

"Your request to return to rescue the remaining survivors of the *Helena* has been refused by the admiral. It is impossible for me to describe how proud I am of you. That is all."

He walked across the pilothouse and out on the wings of the bridge. As he sat down on his bench he could see Smith on the fantail spreading a large blanket on the deck. He knew the daily ritual and could guess what was coming next. The oblong box with the two heavy dumbbells, then the careful exercises. One . . . two . . . three . . . bend . . . crouch . . . up. . . . That boy certainly was keeping himself in condition.

His eye caught Dr. Manchester walking below him on the forecastle, a skipping rope hung from his arm.

"Don't trip, Doc," he called. The doctor looked up and grinned. MacDonald slumped wearily on the bench. He could hear the whispering of the sea as it slid along the *O'Bannon's* sides. In the pilothouse Lieutenant Philip and some of the officers were talking. The murmur of their voices came out to him faintly. The hurried quivering of the *O'Bannon* told him she had caught the scent of home.

10 SURFACE ACTION OFF KOLOMBANGARA ISLAND

THERE WERE JUST a few minutes of twilight left when Captain MacDonald stepped through the open doors of the pilothouse onto the wings of the bridge. Taking a deep breath, he looked over the side. The seas, he noticed, never changed. All day they lay quiet, brooding in the scorching afternoon; reflecting the plush-green jungle of the Solomons. Tonight the slopes and hollows of their swells were a dusky blue, their crests white and lambent. In the west a deep range of clouds rose from the sea, colored an angry red by the setting sun.

Since the Battle of Kula Gulf one week before, the *O'Bannon* had had steady twenty-four-hour-a-day duty. With the destroyers *Radford*, *DeHaven*, and *Nicholas*, she composed a hard-hitting striking force under the command of Captain Bob Briscoe. Their assignments were many: bombard the enemy's positions on Guadalcanal; nightly steam up the Slot, sweeping for Jap task forces that might try to sneak down from Bougainville's or Rabaul's anchorages; escort supply and troop ships; screen mine-laying operations; and take part in anti-submarine patrols.

MacDonald stared at the beauty of the night without seeing it. There were other things on his mind, like the old CPO who had come to his cabin that morning. MacDonald remembered him when he had first come aboard at the Bath Iron Works. He was a powerful, rugged man. But in the last month he had changed. His solid frame drooped. His hair was streaked with gray. His cheeks hung in flabby folds. His hands trembled, he blinked continually. He wept when he spoke to MacDonald. He was cracking up, he said. He couldn't stand the strain any longer. He could not sleep. Food refused to stay on his stomach. He must be transferred. He was afraid he was going to snap.

MacDonald looked out across the *O'Bannon's* slender bow pushing aside the sea. He recalled how he tried to calm the old CPO.

"Try to control yourself, Chief," he said. "We're all tired. But we have to go on."

The reply of the chief rang in his ears.

"We're here until we are dead, Captain."

With nothing but the small, confining ship, the endless glare of the brassy sea, the never-changing lush jungle, the same faces, the same tension, the nightly, nerve-shattering trips up the Slot with sudden death somewhere just in front of you out there in the darkness, MacDonald himself wondered how much longer any of them could stand it.

The increasing tension of the ship seemed to concentrate on his shoulders more every day. His sleep had developed now into mere catnaps with his head resting on the arm of the chair while the *O'Bannon* moved up the Slot. A few days ago he had examined himself closely in a mirror. His hair, he noticed, was thickly trimmed with silver.

In the daytime, from the wings of the bridge where he was now standing, MacDonald could watch his men. He could see them getting thinner, their faces becoming drawn, their eyes sinking deeper into the caves of their skulls. Their dungarees were worn at the knees from wear and bleached from constant washing. Shoes that couldn't be replaced wore out. In the wardroom, Ensign Creigh was constantly being accused of using the last magazine from the States to cover the holes in his shoes.

Pappy Rowland, himself not quite so plump, reported to MacDonald several times that the men were not eating.

"They just push away their plates, Captain," he said. "Food seems to be the last thing they're thinking of."

"Plan the best menus you can, Rowland," MacDonald would tell him wearily. "Do the best you can. Try and tempt them to eat."

Pappy would reply with an "Aye, aye, sir," and get back to his galley, where he would bellow at the messmen and bang around his pots and pans until he felt up to the nightly exchange of scuttlebutt in the chief's quarters.

Tonight they were again on their way up the Slot. The land drive for Munda was starting to get underway. Landings had been made on Enogai Inlet, and the Japs there wiped out. Earlier, the *O'Bannon* had escorted supplies to Rice Anchorage, and as she was about to leave to head back to Tulagi, word had been received of a large Japanese task force headed south.

Rear Admiral Ainsworth immediately ordered his force up the Slot. The column consisted of thirteen ships, among them the cruisers *Honolulu, St. Louis, HMAS Leander* (replacing the lost *Helena*), and the destroyers *O'Bannon, Nicholas, Radford*, and the *Gwin*.

Just before the sun set MacDonald gave his nightly talk.

"Men, this is your captain," he told them. "I know you are weary and exhausted from the strain. But tonight I must call upon you again. Only last week you men fought a gallant battle. Undoubtedly you will see action tonight. We are going up to try and intercept a Jap force. We haven't much information on their strength. We will meet them and I know we will beat them. General Quarters will be at 2300. That is all."

He turned around and told Lieutenant Simmons, who stood on the wings of the bridge:

"Bill, make sure the guns are ready and take the gun bloomers (coverings) off."

"Aye, aye, sir," Simmons said.

Night fell quickly. It was calm, with the moon in its last quarter. Visibility was good. After dinner Rivers, as usual, climbed to the pilothouse with MacDonald's thermos of hot coffee.

At 2300 General Quarters was sounded. Chief Fahrbach, with a quiet, "Good evening, Captain," took his cross-legged position under the chart table. A half-hour later the lookout called.

"Enemy planes off the starboard bow . . . They have running lights . . ."

Jap planes began tracking the force, hanging like droning vultures above the ships at a safe distance of 10,000 to 12,000 yards. Flares were dropped, and the boys on deck idly watched the red, green, and white lights bobbing in the sea. This was a nightly occurrence, and even curiosity had long died away. Two firemen who had received permission to go topside sprawled alongside the fireroom hatch humming "Me and My Shadow."

The force continued to move along at about twenty-five knots, hugging the shoreline until the ships were formless shadows. In the pilothouse Ensign Creigh leaned against the rolling bulkhead by the radio set and told himself there was nothing he hated more than this tropical heat. When the ship left Tulagi and hatches were dogged down for action, the heat of the day was shut in the ship. Even at night it choked you. Would he ever see those skiing days at Dartmouth again? Cold, biting wind whistled about your ears as you sailed over the snow. "God, when this damn war is over," he told himself, "this sailor is going to buy a ranch in Montana, and do nothing but hunt, fish, and raise horses. Now take that place out in . . ."

The phone buzzed.

"Bridge," he answered. He listened for a moment, hung up, and turned to MacDonald.

"Captain, there's a Jap force of five destroyers and one cruiser, course 128, in position off Kolombangara headed for our direction."

"Thanks, John." MacDonald grinned to himself. Probably the only thing that would make old John lift his voice would be a snowstorm, he thought.

Over the ship's telephone he repeated Creigh's message to Simmons, the gunnery officer, and added, "Maybe we'll have some more fun tonight, Bill."

"We're ready, Captain," Simmons answered.

As MacDonald sat back in his chair, it suddenly came to him they would meet the Japs some time in the early hours of the morning. It would be July 13. The Battle of Guadalcanal had been fought on the Thirteenth. There had been thirteen ships in Callaghan's force. He rapidly counted the ships tonight. Thirteen. Now once again the number 13 was appearing. "It might be a lucky omen," he thought.

As the destroyer drew near the Jap column the ships formed in battle disposition. Torpedoes were readied. The *O'Bannon* took her position astern of the *Nicholas*, who was flying the flag of Captain McInerney, the destroyer squadron leader. Astern of the *O'Bannon* were the *Taylor*, the *Radford*, and the *Jenkins*. Cruisers followed, and then a second squadron of destroyers, led by the *Gwin*, under the command of Captain Ryan. At midnight the *Radford* reported engine trouble and left the group temporarily.

Although it was now overcast, the sky was fused with shafts of brilliant moonlight. The sea was still calm but a slight northwest breeze had sprung up.

The cruiser *Honolulu* spotted the Japs:

"Angel to Sugar: We have enemy estimated as six ships."

The flagship replied:

"Sugar to Angel: Keep them in sight. Speed up."

The ships moved in closer. Later Captain Ryan called:

"Devil to Sugar: I see them bearing three-one-zero." And the order came back again:

"Sugar to Devil: Keep them in sight."

The ships cut steadily through the sea. The freshening breeze had washed clear the face of the sky and the moon hung clear in the heavens. At 0145 the cruiser *St. Louis* called:

"Cupid to Sugar: We are crossing his bow."

MacDonald called to Torpedo Officer Mitchell: "Train on target . . . Stand by to fire . . .", and down at the torpedo tubes, men tensed as the echo came to them—"Stand by." Speed and bearings of the Jap ships were dialed into the torpedo control on the starboard bridge wing.

"Aye, aye, Captain." The voice sounded thin in the night air.

A dark column of silhouettes loomed off the *O'Bannon's* starboard bow; then starboard beam at 6,000 yards. Seconds passed, and the flagship called:

"Sugar to TF: Fire torpedoes."

Torpedo Officer Mitchell's commands snapped like a lash:

"Fire one . . . fire two . . . fire three . . ." Each time he called a small blue light flashed in front of his control board and a large steel fish swished away from the deck, as the two columns passed each other in the silent blackness. Suddenly a Jap searchlight flickered on. At his smoke-watch post Finley was again describing the action for the men below.

"Their searchlights are on . . . Gee, I feel just like a guy on a stage."

"The hell with that," Zimmerman shouted from the fireroom. "What's happening?"

"We're going in again," Finley replied. "There go Four and Five tubes. Christ, they're walking their shells around us." The Jap guns had opened up as the destroyers roared in for the torpedo attack. Great watery spouts moved toward the *O'Bannon.*

MacDonald, shielding his face from the intense white glare of the searchlight, shouted to Simmons:

"Bill, get the searchlight."

The *O'Bannon* lifted to the recoil of her five-inch rifles. Salvo after salvo followed each other straight down that beam of light. The light vanished. A second later the torpedoes struck home. The hull of the second Jap ship of the line, a cruiser later identified as a Zintsu class, grew a dull red like the lid of an overheated stove. Steel sides glowed until the plates were almost a light pink. Then, as if the inferno could no longer be confined, the ship burst apart in one horrifying gust of flame. On the smoke watch Finley, awestruck, stammered:

"Good God, Zip, her searchlight was blown about 500 feet in the air." Then he added, almost unbelievingly, "There's nothing left of her—she's—she's gone."

In the meantime the guns of the cruisers *Honolulu, St. Louis,* and *Leander* had engaged the rest of the Jap line. The heavy ships were shrouded in glowing smoke spitting great flashes of fire as each salvo left their fifteen eight-inch guns. Once the *Leander's* searchlight flickered off and on, and her guns stopped as she dropped out of the battle formation off the *O'Bannon's* port beam. She blinked. She had been hit by a torpedo. Over the TBS Ainsworth ordered the *Radford:*

"Sugar to Sweetheart: Sissy is hurt. Stand by her."

"Sweetheart to Sugar: I see her off starboard now. Proceeding to assist."

As the *Radford* moved over to the damaged *Leander* the Jap destroyers on the tail end of their battle line turned and fled. Ainsworth barked over the TBS to Captain McInerney:

"Sugar to Honey: Don't let those bastards get away."

McInerney answered:

"Honey to Sugar: Don't worry. We'll polish them off if we can catch up with them."

At McInerney's commands over the TBS the *O'Bannon* and the *Nicholas* swung about. The two destroyers raced after the fleeing Japs with engines full, sending up curtains of spray high in the air as they charged through the sea. But the Japs had too much of a start. In a few minutes they melted away in the darkness.

On their way back to join the other ships MacDonald spotted the burning hulks of the Jap destroyers and the cruiser he had hit. He called to the *Nicholas* over the TBS:

"Candy to Honey: Let's take care of this junk," and the *Nicholas* answered: "Honey to Candy: Good idea."

MacDonald spoke to his gunnery officer, "Get those burning ships, Bill, and give them all you've got," and to his torpedo officer, "Same with you, Mitch."

As they circled the blazing Jap men-of-war the *Nicholas* and the *O'Bannon* fired salvos and torpedoes until the gulf rocked with thunder. Showers of flame and oil covered the sea. One Jap destroyer made a half circle after receiving a spread of torpedoes, then gave a frantic lurch, turned over on her side, and sank. As the Jap slid under its magazines were touched off, and a fiery bubble, red from the inferno within, rose over the spot. The Jap cruiser hit earlier by the *O'Bannon* was now upside down, and MacDonald and his officers could see the silhouette of her long, black hull. Several salvos tore through her bottom, and with a scream of tortured steel she split in half and went under in a frenzy of exploding depth charges and hissing boilers.

While the *O'Bannon* and *Nicholas* were administering their death blows, a second group of Jap destroyers appeared and attacked Captain Ryan's supporting squadron of destroyers coming up from the rear of the battle line. Ships milled about in the blackness. Searchlights flickered on and off. Friend and foe looked alike. The *O'Bannon* and the *Nicholas* swept into the battle. All about them guns were disgorging flame and destruction. The attacking Jap line was swinging about hard, almost standing on their fantails. After a hurried hit-and-run torpedo attack some of the ships in Captain Ryan's group were hit. Some lay helpless in the water while their sister ships made frantic radical turns to avoid collisions while still firing at the fleeing Jap ships. The TBS shouted one code name after the other.

"Cupid to Angel: Where are you?"

"Angel to Cupid: We are hit."

"Candy to Honey: Where is Sugar?"

"Honey to Sweetheart: Who is missing?"

"Devil to Candy: I am going to illuminate."

"Honey to Candy: Who is that on your port hand?"

"Candy to Honey: Devil. She will illuminate."

The words had just left MacDonald's lips when there was a tremendous flash on the *O'Bannon's* bow.

"That's the *Gwin*," shouted Lieutenant Philip. "She's hit."

Ainsworth called to McInerney over the TBS: "Sugar to Honey: Are all your boys accounted for?"

McInerney reported: "Honey to Sugar: All present and accounted for."

He then asked Captain Ryan: "Sugar to Devil: Are your boys accounted for?"

The reply was: "Devil to Sugar: We are hit. We are pulling out."

"Sugar to TF: Retire."

The cruisers swung into line with the *Nicholas, Radford,* and *O'Bannon* in screening positions as all ships steamed out of Kula Gulf, headed back to Tulagi. Several destroyers in Captain Ryan's squadron had been hit by the torpedoes of the second column of Jap destroyers and damaged. The *Honolulu, St. Louis,* and *Leander* were damaged.

Lieutenant Noonan on the bridge, watching the crippled ships limping home, turned to Dr. Manchester, a grin stretching from ear to ear.

"You know, Doc," he chuckled, "all the cruisers will be out of business, so from now on we'll be the 'big boys' and maybe Halsey will throw us a couple of minesweepers to do our screening."

The next day the damaged cruisers returned to the Navy yard for repairs. Some would be out of action for months. The tiny tin-can fleet now stood alone in the Battle of the Solomons.

11 RESCUE OF THE *HELENA* SURVIVORS

"WELL," MACDONALD THOUGHT, "at last it's been decided. We're to be the expendables tonight . . . but it seems ironical that after all these nights she might go down without firing a shot . . . at least she should be allowed to go down fighting . . ."

Sitting in the stern of his gig now cutting through the glassy sea toward the *O'Bannon* hanging on the hook in the Tulagi anchorage, MacDonald was going over the plan outlined to him a few minutes before by Rear Admiral Ainsworth at the conference aboard the *Nicholas*.

The *Helena* survivors were to be rescued. Word had been received a week before that 175 survivors, including MacDonald's close friend, Commander Jack Chew, had reached Jap-held Vella Lavella approximately two hundred miles from their base. The information told how the *Helena's* men had paddled rafts and rubber boats right to the Jap-held beach where they met up with friendly natives who sheltered and fed them while enemy patrols searched the jungle.

Their rescue would be a difficult one. Up to this time no ship had penetrated that deep into the gulf. The area was less than thirty miles away from the powerful Japanese naval base in the Shortland Islands, from which a task force could swoop down and destroy them in a few minutes. The shore bristled with tremendous fire power of heavy shore batteries, while Jap planes continually patrolled the area. While ships stole under the cover of darkness to the rescue area, someone had to stay offshore as bait for any task forces, enemy planes, or suspicious shore installations. The rescue operations would take several hours. The ship to be sacrificed was *not* to fire back at attacking planes for fear of attracting surface units or submarines which might spot the rescue ships and bottle them up in the gulf. She would just have to sit and take it. That ship was to be the *O'Bannon*.

Although a comfortable breeze which had swooped over Tulagi to race across the water was now filling out his shirt, MacDonald could feel a clammy sweat as he rubbed a hand across his forehead. The gig had now reached the *O'Bannon's* side. The coxswain held fast to the Jacob's ladder and looked expectantly at his captain, but MacDonald was staring out at the other destroyers at anchor. The water slapped against the *O'Bannon's* side and the whaleboat rocked gently. The coxswain coughed, and MacDonald, startled, looked up. He rose to his feet and grabbed at the ladder. He could feel the rough rope rub against his palms. He was still thinking as he walked to his cabin, "We can't get away with it tonight. There's a law of averages somewhere . . ."

Late that afternoon he outlined the plan to his officers. The task force that night, MacDonald told them, was to be composed of the *Nicholas*, the *Radford*, the *Jenkins*, and the *O'Bannon* under Captain Thomas J. Ryan and Captain Francis X. McInerney. The *Nicholas* would act as their flagship. The *O'Bannon* would precede the main force. She was to be the "bait" while Captain Ryan's force screened the rescue operation by APD's (old-age destroyers converted into transports).

The *O'Bannon* got underway at the usual time. After clearing the Tulagi anchorage, MacDonald addressed his crew.

"Men, this is your captain," he told them. "Tonight we are going on a mission that might be called dangerous. I hope we will not see any action tonight. This is one night we are not looking for any trouble. We are going to take part in this operation. You will probably be up all night and I know you will stand it willingly in view of the mission we are about to perform. General Quarters will be sounded at 2100. Take plenty of water because it will be a long, hard night. That is all."

Captain MacDonald looked at Lieutenant Simmons. "Your orders are not to fire, Bill, even if we are attacked."

The gunnery officer opened his mouth to speak, but as he met Captain MacDonald's steady gaze the words died before they passed his lips. All he said was, "Aye, aye, Captain."

And on the deck weary boys cheered MacDonald. What the hell, weren't they going in to rescue the guys from the *Helena?* If they had been left out of the operation the morale of the *O'Bannon* would have sunk below sea level.

She moved up the Slot. Chiefs and crew members lay about her deck, sleeping or talking—the favorite pastime aboard ship. In the radio shack Chief Padgett and his first class radioman, Guess, picked up their nightly discussion of the automobile business they would some day own in Washington. The plans of the partnership had been drawn. The location had been selected. They would sell Fords. "Greatest car on the road today, George," insisted Padgett, who had some experience in automobile salesmanship, while Guess would nod solemnly. Then they would go into details, from the color of the upholstery to the last bolt on the crankcase. Automobiles exhausted, they switched to their next favorite subject: the last night they spent in Boston with their wives. It was in a hotel. The dinner had been carefully planned. George was at his best, and there was plenty of laughter. The hours flew. Then came the last toast:

"To the *O'Bannon.*" The cocktails were drunk slowly. Then they left quietly. A last kiss. A firm squeeze and a whispered "Good luck, honey," and the two men walked back to their ships.

Then Padgett would talk about his daughter Carol, and he would unconsciously twist the light identification bracelet on his wrist she had given him. Their conversation usually died away at 10 P.M. They would sit in silence, each man occupied with things dear to him; thoughts too intimate to say aloud.

One thing was never forgotten. The letter each had written—

"in case we get it"—to his wife. When General Quarters sounded and the ship readied for battle, one of them would say with studied nonchalance: "Well, here we go again—don't forget that letter."

In the fire control room Bess and his crew listened to Fire Controlman Third Class Joe Ball. A tall, round-shouldered man in his early thirties, he had been a former miner in a southern coal town. Throughout the ship he seemed to be the only man not affected by the long nerve-shattering patrols. Most of his early life had been spent chipping coal in small damp holes in lonely mountain mines. When the tension was bad and men grew tense, Ball would tell them with a grin:

"What the hell are you worrying about? How would you like to be down in a pit, never knowing when the son of a bitch was going to cave in on you?"

And in the crew's quarters young Cianca, with one arm around a bunk chain to steady himself against the rolling of the ship, was rereading for the twentieth time a letter from his mother. She never could understand, she wrote, how he got in the Navy when he was only sixteen. Don't they have to have the parents' consent? And Cianca would grin as he recalled how he had left his school books on the front porch on his way to the recruiting office, after he had hidden his mother's glasses and nonchalantly got her to sign "some papers"—"Just formal papers, Mom, so I can go to work this summer and earn some spare change."

Finally, at 2100 General Quarters sounded and men and officers took their battle stations.

On deck they cursed the large "bomber's moon" sailing along in a cloudless sky. The *O'Bannon* was steaming along steadily, silent except for the purring of the engine and the whining blowers.

At 2200 a lookout shouted, "Flashing white light off starboard bow."

A small white light blinked through MacDonald's binoculars. It seemed to be sending some type of SOS. Over the TBS he told Captain McInerney:

"Jack to Jill: We make out a small whaleboat. Looks like survivors." And the answer came back immediately:

"Jill to Jack: Can't stop. Mark location. On our way back in the morning we will investigate."

"On our way back," MacDonald echoed to himself. "If we come back."

A half-hour later, Jap planes spotted the ships. They moved above the *O'Bannon*, watching but never coming within range. Once several flares exploded, floating down off the bow. "Anything can happen now, Captain," Philip said, and MacDonald nodded grimly.

Kolombangara slid by in the moonlight, and the *O'Bannon* moved deeper into enemy territory. Finally Vella Lavella loomed up on her porthand for the first time. She moved still deeper into the gulf. The rescue ships had disappeared for their rendezvous with the survivors in the darkness. The *O'Bannon* was now less than thirty miles from the Jap naval base in the Shortland Islands. The other destroyers under Captain Ryan had moved in to screen the rescue operations. The *O'Bannon* was now alone on the sacrificial altar.

At 0100 the Japanese planes, still droning overhead, heaved in for the attack. Three large bombers screamed down. The bridge sprang into action. At MacDonald's shouted commands the *O'Bannon* swung hard to port. Lieutenant Burford could hear the wail of the falling stick of bombs. A daisy cutter hit the water. It exploded on contact with a dazzling flash of flame—at approximately the spot where the *O'Bannon* had been the moment before.

Steel fragments sang through the air. Men topside hugged the decks. Another and another followed. Soon the sea about her sides was blossoming with bomb blasts and geysers of water.

At MacDonald's commands, Quartermaster Gotschall swung the helm furiously in frantic evasive action.

An hour passed. The Japs kept up a continuous attack. Several times Lieutenant Simmons up in the director called down to Captain MacDonald, pleading,

"I got solutions on them all over the place, Captain. When can I shoot? They're coming close . . ."

But MacDonald always shouted, "Hold your fire."

Once after a bomb had landed close enough to send spray flying across the topside, MacDonald called the flagship:

"Jack to Jill: They're coming close. Can we fire?"

But the answer was brief.

"Jill to Jack: Hold your fire."

The hours dragged on like centuries. More Jap planes joined the attack. The planes zoomed so low the officers on the bridge could hear the scream of the bombs as they fell and would automatically duck as they hit. Several times delayed-action fuses went off under the surface of the sea, sending up gushers of water, tinged with dull red fire.

At 0300 MacDonald, clinging to the rail of the bridge during a lull in the attack, turned to Pfeifer and said:

"God, Carl, now I know what Christ suffered in Gethsemane. I swear I'm sweating blood now."

"And every man in the ship feels the same, Captain," the officer answered.

The *O'Bannon* was under steady bombing for five hours. Several times sticks of bombs exploded so close the destroyer shook from stem to stern and it seemed certain her plates must give. Even Finley on the smoke watch failed to give his rapid-fire account of the happenings. The explosions were coming so frequently and close he was forced to hug the deck. Repair parties were constantly reporting to the bridge:

". . . And no damage in Repair Three, sir . . ."

Finally at 0500 MacDonald asked the flagship:

"Jack to Jill: These bastards are coming too close. Can we fire now?" Again the answer was:

"Jill to Jack: Hold your fire." But at 0530 the TBS barked:

"Jill to Jack: Mission accomplished. Hit the next bastard that comes near."

Two more planes were coming in for an attack. They were confident now. This was easy . . .

But now Bess in fire control was snarling the range and bearings. On the 20-mm. guns exhausted, sweating men waited. The planes came down closer. Every gun on the ship opened up. Tracers flew up from the ship and clawed at the planes. The Jap pilots were surprised. They spun their ships about and pulled out of their dives, their bombs exploding far off the *O'Bannon's* bow. The flickering tracers mowed their tails. Refusing to renew their attacks they zoomed off and sped away.

The guns stopped. About the ship men slumped at their battle stations, tasting the salt of their sweat and wondering why their hands shook as if with the palsy.

In the darkness on the bridge MacDonald whispered a quiet prayer, and Finley on the smoke watch said wearily, "We're going home now."

The men stood at battle stations until daybreak when they passed Kolombangara. Turning to Pfeifer, MacDonald said:

"The boys have never seen it by daylight, Carl. Suppose you tell them about it now." Pfeifer, walking to the ship's mike, said:

"Men, this is your executive officer. We are passing Kolombangara on the starboard. That's the place you've been bombarding and haven't had a chance to see in the daytime."

The boys watched the low hump-backed land mass slip by. Morning mists were still rising from the jungle, and the entire scene looked to be shrouded by a heavy fog. Some wondered if Jap lookouts could see their ship and speculated as to the thoughts running through their minds.

Just before the *O'Bannon* left Kula Gulf, a lookout reported, "Object in the water dead ahead . . . looks like a man hanging on a log."

MacDonald moved to the wings of the bridge, and through the circle of the glasses he could see several men clinging to logs and shattered rafts. Some had pieces of canvas over their heads to protect them from the sun. All appeared to be stark naked.

"Pass the word to the boatswains to stand by to pick up survivors," MacDonald ordered, and Chief Boatswain's Mate Charles Picton lowered a Jacob's ladder and stood by with life rings. The *O'Bannon* slowed her speed as she drew near, and the men on her decks could see small brown men, completely naked, huddled alongside logs and splintered spars. Several started to swim away.

Picton shouted, "Grab this . . ." as he threw the life rings over the side. One Jap punched it aside, left his log, and swam away. Two others calmly pushed the bobbing life ring aside and stared up at the sailors on the deck with blank, brown faces. MacDonald asked the flagship: "Jack to Jill: Shall we stand by to pick up these survivors?"

"Jill to Jack: Our job is to get the *Helena* survivors back to base. Let them go," was the reply.

The *O'Bannon* swung about and joined the other ships. An hour later the lookout again reported, "Whaleboat off port bow."

It was the location marked by MacDonald the night before when his lookout had first reported a light blinking. Now through his glasses he could make out two Japs squatting in the bottom of a boat. The *Radford* was ordered to investigate, and as she moved close some of her crew swung from a Jacob's ladder and tried to get the Japs to climb aboard.

This time there was no hesitation. Both men grabbed the ladder and were helped on deck. A few days later MacDonald learned that the Japs had been survivors of the cruiser sunk by the *O'Bannon*.

Back at Tulagi that afternoon the happy, shoeless, tattered *Helena* survivors were transferred from the ships to the base hospital. Early the next day MacDonald visited Commander Jack Chew, who had been released from the hospital and was resting in the officers' club, bandaged feet propped up on a chair in front of him.

"From the coral, Mac," he said, pointing. "My feet feel like I've been walking on a street paved with razor blades."

In reply to his eager questioning, MacDonald outlined the night's operation. Chew shook his head.

"We certainly owe a lot to all you fellows, Mac. I hope we have a chance to repay you sometime."

"But what happened after the *Helena* was hit, Jack?" Mac-Donald asked. "Were you hurt? Did . . ."

Chew laughed. "I'll start from the beginning," he said.

"The *Helena* went down, Mac, at approximately 0130. When daylight came the survivors were more or less scattered around, clinging to various life rafts, and they seemed to be in about three different groups. One of the groups was with Captain Cecil, commanding officer of the *Helena*. They had a motorboat left by the *Nicholas* with Ensign Jack Fitch, son of Admiral Fitch, as the boat officer. The boat towed Captain Cecil's life rafts to New Georgia Island. My group of about 165 men was drifting toward the islands, and we were afraid that we would drift down onto Kolombangara where the Japs were. For three days we drifted back and forth. For several days Jap Zero planes would take a look at us but didn't do anything. We had very little water and some food which was secured to the boats and we rationed this out. Each time we drifted near an island and drifted away some of the men gave up. Never before had I seen men just give up and die. In my life raft there was a young reserve officer, a large fellow and very powerful. On the third day when we drifted fairly close to Vella Lavella we started paddling in order to make the island and we all took turns. We were worn out and didn't seem to be making much progress against the tide but this officer kept paddling furiously. We finally reached Vella Lavella. We knew the Japs were in Kolombangara and Vella Lavella but we didn't know just exactly where. When we reached shore we expected to be mowed down by machine-gun fire. We drifted very close to a Japanese barge. Many more survivors followed and drifted ashore. As they tried to walk they fell. Their feet had become horribly swollen from the water and were cut by coral. Our first thought was to get the food on the rafts.

"We were awakened by someone trying to tear up the food on the rafts. It was a Jap. We went after him and killed him with our knives which were all we had. We expected any moment that the Japs would come down on us so we took to the woods. Some of the natives came down and took us into the mountains.

They hid us in caves and doctored us up and fed us the best they could. I was never so glad to eat native food—anything would have tasted good.

"We were covered with oil and our hair had stiffened. I had a handlebar mustache and couldn't drink any water and enjoy it because it tasted of oil—never again will I raise a mustache! The beards of some of the boys stiffened up too and they didn't enjoy the food or water. We made preparations to defend ourselves against the Japanese on the island.

"I was the senior officer and later found out that there was another group of survivors on another point of the island and a young supply officer was the senior one in that group. Through the assistance of the natives we sent a messenger down and organized plans to get off the island.

"The original plan was to get us off prior to the sixteenth but that had to be called off. We were completely heartbroken when we realized the date had been set back. But finally another date was set—last night. When the fateful day came we were afraid that the Japs might discover our moving from the hills to the beach. Then when the planes dropped flares over your group we were scared to death and felt this was the end. We thought the Japs had come out to finish us off because we were exposed.

"The natives were wonderful. They even helped us get our boats down to the beach and rowed us to our destroyers. I gave them the only thing of value I had—my revolver—and they were overjoyed. What a small price, Mac, to pay for what those people did for us."

While Captain MacDonald was listening to Commander Chew, Dr. Manchester was at the Tulagi's base hospital talking to a chief petty officer, a survivor of the destroyer *Strong*. Manchester had been seeking the young officer who had sat next to him at the baseball game at Noumea.

Yes, the chief told Dr. Manchester, he knew that officer.

"Was he one of the survivors taken to Australia?" the physician asked eagerly.

"I'm sorry, sir," the chief said, "he went down with the ship."

12 AUCKLAND—PAPPY GETS HIS FOOD SUPPLY

TWO DAYS AFTER the *Helena* survivors had been rescued and sent ashore to the hospital, the *O'Bannon* and her remaining sisters of the Solomons' tin-can fleet, the *Nicholas* and the *Radford*, joined forces with Rear Admiral Crutchley of the Australian Royal Navy and his two cruisers—the *Australian* and the *Hobart*—flying his flag, to form a task force.

For several days the force patrolled the Slot. The battle for the control of New Georgia was still in a critical stage, with heavy Japanese forces bivouacked in the Kolombangara vicinity. Several times the task force steamed through the darkness to meet heavy Japanese surface units moving down from the north to molest the Marines and Army troops on Munda or New Georgia, but always at the last minute, like the phantom ship of Kula Gulf, the Japs vanished in the blackness.

Less than two weeks after the force had been formed, the *Australian* was attacked and damaged by a Jap torpedo. The force had been zigzagging at high speed when the cruiser was hit. The *O'Bannon*, on her starboard side, immediately swung about to her aid. Although the *Australian* had been badly hit, she signaled she was able to return to Espiritu Santo, under the escort of the *O'Bannon*.

The *Radford* and the *Nicholas* stayed with the *Hobart* and attempted to find the submarine which, it was later determined, had successfully escaped under heavy depth bombing.

After escorting the wounded cruiser back to Espiritu Santo,

MacDonald paid his respects to Rear Admiral Crutchley, a tall, distinguished man with a reddish-brown goatee.

When he returned to the *O'Bannon*, MacDonald was grinning.

"We have just been detailed to escort a convoy from New Zealand to the Canal with the *Chevalier*. We'll get underway first thing in the morning," he told the officers.

At 0600 the *O'Bannon* and the *Chevalier* left for New Zealand. An hour later MacDonald was standing before the ship's loudspeaker talking to his men:

". . . And so we are going to proceed to Auckland to pick up convoy. If at all possible I will give you leave ashore while we are there. All you boys deserve it. That is all."

The officers waited anxiously to reach Auckland. They were beginning to feel the restlessness of the crew. It moved like an electric current through the ship, sometimes exploding. At simple remarks boys would curse their shipmates, hurling bitter, stinging taunts, or would spring at each other, fists flying in sudden bursts of fury they never could explain later. Others would mill about, growling: "Break it up . . . break it up . . . ya want Pfeifer down here?"

But these fist fights were explosive, secret affairs that never passed beyond the bulkheads of the crew's quarters. An officer might see a discolored eye or split lip, but the boy would grin cheerfully when questioned, insisting,

"It's nothing, sir, just a fall against the ladder . . . Nothing at all, sir."

The three-day cruise to Auckland would do much to ease the tenseness of the ship. To Dr. Manchester, the trip was a chance to catch up on more wood carving. Each time they hit Tulagi, or any of the anchorages in the Solomons, Dr. Manchester would return late in the evening, his arms laden with all types of native wood. It wasn't long before he had carved a beautiful dinner set and a cigarette box, complete with a handle of tiny "boo-boo" shells picked up on the beach at Tulagi. The day Lieutenant Noonan caught the doctor emptying his pockets of the brilliantly colored shells, Noonan, always on the alert for a nickname, immediately changed Dr. Manchester's from "Tecumseh" to "Boo-Boo."

The day before the *O'Bannon* reached Auckland, Captain MacDonald called Pappy Rowland to the bridge.

"Chief, we haven't had any fresh vegetables for a long time," he said. "In fact it's been nearly a year." He cleared his throat and said in a confidential tone:

"Do you think you might be able to get some in Auckland?"

Pappy grinned:

"I'll try, Captain," and MacDonald said briskly:

"As soon as we dock, Rowland, jump over to the commissary officer's office and see what can be done."

"Aye, aye, sir," Rowland said and left the bridge, his eyes twinkling behind his glasses.

The *O'Bannon* docked early the next morning on July 24. A half-hour earlier, as she passed the flagship of the convoy, the commodore had signaled:

"Prepare to leave as soon as you are fueled."

On the *O'Bannon* sullen men leaned against the ship's lifeline and gloomily watched the few people passing along the dock. This was a Sunday morning, and the quiet little port with its clean white brick buildings was nearly deserted. Except MacDonald, who had to call on the commodore of the convoy, Pappy Rowland was the only man to leave the ship.

"We have just forty-five minutes to fuel and get provisions aboard, Rowland," MacDonald warned him, "so you'll have to work fast."

Pappy hurried off the *O'Bannon* toward the commissary office. Before he entered the squat, white building at the end of the pier, he button-holed a guard who had just come out the door.

"Pardon me," Pappy asked, "do you happen to know the name of the commissary officer here?"

The guard scratched his head. "Yes," he said, "I think his last name is . . ."

Rowland waved his hand. "Never mind his last name. Do you know his first name?"

The guard's face brightened. "Why yes, his name is Tom. But why do . . ."

But Pappy was already through the door and walking down the hall to the commissary office.

He passed some stenographers and entered a small, private office. A short, stubby man who had been staring out of the window across the harbor, looked up. Pappy saluted briskly.

"Rowland, chief commissary from the *O'Bannon*. Just docked, sir."

Then Pappy stopped. He squinted his eyes.

"Could your first name be Tom, sir?" he asked.

The officer nodded. Rowland snapped his fingers.

"That's where I heard of you, sir," he said, "one day out in the chief's club in Noumea. One of the *Honolulu's* chiefs told me about you."

The officer scowled slightly. "And what did he say about me?"

Rowland grinned. "Nothing, sir, except that every man on his ship wanted to step right up and kiss you when they left here last time. In the chief's club he talked about you for an hour . . ."

The commissary officer, bruised and battered by complaints for months, thawed. He smiled, and then Pappy fired his secret weapon.

"I took the liberty of bringing you a couple of cigars, sir," he said, "I hope you won't mind," as he brought out several of Bess's cigars—saved by Pappy's careful planning from the splurge of celebrating his new son.

A half-hour later Pappy walked nonchalantly aboard the *O'Bannon*. The whole ship was on the lookout for him, from Captain MacDonald down to the last man of the crew lounging on the deck. His chief's hat was perched jauntily on the side of his head and one of Bess's cigars stuck in the corner of his mouth. Behind came several longshoremen with small trucks, piled high with crates of onions, carrots, lettuce, and—the eyes of the crew bulged—a small crate of strawberries.

On board Pappy waved aside any and all questions. "Nothing to it," he said. "Nothing to it."

The convoy of our large transports, jammed to the gunwales with American troops, and guarded by the *O'Bannon* and the *Chevalier*, cleared Auckland at 1030 that same morning. The day was balmy. Men and officers relaxed to dream of home, and soon Auckland's neatly trimmed lawns and white buildings faded in the distance.

That night, July 25, before dinner had cleared, a strawberry shortcake was placed in front of MacDonald. It was his thirty-fifth birthday. As usual in the Navy, the birthdays of all the officers are carefully checked in the Navy Directory when they come aboard and placed on the calendar. As the Captain bent over to cut the cake, Ensign Burford was startled to notice his Captain's hair was almost completely silver.

With the transports delivered safely, the *O'Bannon* moved on to Noumea for minor repairs. The recreations were few. There was still work to be done. Rust spots that seemed to appear over-night must be chipped and painted, brass polished, boilers cleaned; the entire ship must be examined with a fine-toothed comb.

At night under the starswept sky the crew would gather on the deck for Ensign "Slim Jim" Garten's movie offerings. There would be groans if it turned out to be a Western and wild cheers if Hedy Lamarr, Betty Grable, or Marlene Dietrich danced across the screen.

Peggy, still limping from her fractured leg which had healed perfectly but was now slightly stiff, was usually seen in her place of honor on the lap of one of the officers.

13 BARGE HUNTING

BY MID-AUGUST the New Georgia Campaign was finished except for minor mopping up operations. Strong Japanese troops were still entrenched on near-by Kolombangara and a campaign there would possibly mean more vicious jungle fighting and digging stubborn Japs from their dugouts and pill-boxes with flame throwers and bayonets.

On the afternoon of August 14 the *O'Bannon*, again in her old place in the Slot-sweeping tin-can fleet, together with the *Nicholas, Taylor, Chevalier*, and *Radford*, escorted a group of troop-laden APD's on the first island-hopping venture of the war. At dawn the southwestern tip of Vella Lavella had been invaded and Kolombangara had been successfully bypassed.

The Jap positions rapidly became precarious. Barges, swinging down from Rabaul and the Shortland Islands to Choiseul and then across to Kolombangara, were the only remaining means of supplying their troops.

For several nights the *O'Bannon* and her sister ships patrolled the vicinity of Vella Lavella trying to intercept the barge traffic. Jap planes harassed the force, attacking for as long as two and a half hours at one time, but no damage was caused. One night, while traveling through Gizo Strait, a narrow, treacherous space of water between Vella Lavella and Gizo Island, several Jap planes pounced on them, bombing the force incessantly. Restricted in their maneuverings, the ships dueled with the diving planes, while bomb splashes rose about them. Other Jap planes joined the attack, and soon a weird conglomeration of float planes, twin-engine bombers, and dive bombers were dropping stick after stick of bombs about the wildly zigzagging ships. Once a near miss exploded off the *O'Bannon's* starboard bow, denting the plates and lifting her out of the sea. Miraculously, there was no damage.

The next morning back at Tulagi, it was estimated that more than eighty bombs had been dropped about the force.

From August 15 to 17 the destroyers escorted reinforcing troop landings. But late afternoon of the seventeenth, as the force was about to retire to Tulagi, information was received of a Jap formation, reported to be composed of many barges and four unidentified ships, headed down from Bougainville.

Captain Ryan immediately ordered his destroyers, the *O'Bannon*, the *Nicholas*, the *Taylor*, and the *Chevalier*, to meet the oncoming Japs, who appeared to be making an attempted reinforcement of their positions on Vella Lavella or Kolombangara. Black Cat pilots preceded Ryan's force as the ships passed Vella Lavella. As darkness set in MacDonald gave his nightly talk to his men, relaying to them what information he had received. Rivers, as usual, brought him his thermos bottle of coffee, and the ship settled down in silence to wait for contact with her enemy. A bright new moon appeared, lighting up the formation. In the pilothouse, sitting cross-legged under his table, Chief Yeoman Fahrbach wrote across the top of his pad, "Tonight is disgustingly clear."

At 2335 a Black Cat pilot reported, "Angel to TF: Four DD's coming down and a number of barges."

A few minutes later the *O'Bannon's* lookout cried, "Enemy planes dead ahead."

Now flares dropped around the ships, exploding about their sides and settling in their wakes. The *Nicholas*, heading the line, was bracketed with bombs. Water shot up about her bow, but she reported no damage. From then on the Japs contented themselves with tracking the formation with flares.

At 0045 the enemy was sighted.

"Contact made, Bill," MacDonald told his gunnery officer, "Get ready."

"All ready, Captain," Simmons answered.

The Jap destroyers bore down steadily, their sleek hulls sheltering countless barges, strung across the sea like ugly black beetles. Overhead the moon continued on her complacent journey, old as mankind itself, across a clear starlit sky. The sea was serene and still. The air hung lifeless about MacDonald and his officers, standing in silence in the *O'Bannon's* pilothouse.

At 0047 the TBS came to life. Captain Ryan on the flagship called:

"Pat to Mike: Japs turning away."

Through his binoculars MacDonald could make out the silhouettes of the Jap destroyers etched against the blackness, heeling about in a sharp turn, fleeing back to Bougainville and deserting the barges that floated helplessly about the moonlit sea.

The Black Cat pilot reported in disgust:

"Angel to TF: Japs running away from their barges."

Captain Ryan immediately ordered his ships:

"Pat to TF: Get those escorts. We can clean up those barges on the way back."

The formation charged through the sea, attempting to head off the Jap destroyers. Several large barges, towing away small ones, appeared on the *O'Bannon's* portside, and as the ships passed large swells threw them high in the air dumping men and cargo into the sea.

The fleeing Japs opened fire, and pillars of sea water rose about the *Nicholas* and the *O'Bannon* as they moved in for a torpedo run. Jap salvos continued to bounce around them and the long, orange tongues licked at the night. But the Japs refused to close the range. Five-inch salvos were brought to bear on them.

Captain Ryan ordered:

"Pat to TF: Open fire."

The guns of the *O'Bannon*, second in line, tore at a large Terutski destroyer outlined against the horizon and flames sprang from her forecastle. Then Jap planes attacked and dove down over the *Nicholas,* showering her with bombs that exploded less than a hundred yards off her starboard side. The *O'Bannon's* guns went into rapid fire and the Jap destroyer kept her ground for a few minutes. Then a salvo from the *O'Bannon* ripped her into shattered, twisted steel that lay burning fiercely in the sea. Flares rode the swells, and through the circle of his glasses MacDonald could see the panorama of battle—twisting ships, oily black smoke pouring from their funnels, the sea split wide with paths of foam, and the lean shapes of the ships spitting flame or engulfed with fire. But the Jap line was fleeing rapidly and soon moved out of range.

"Pat to TF: Let's get the barges now."

The *O'Bannon* and the ships astern of her followed the *Nicholas* as she swung about to charge into the barges, which now lay directly in the line of fire waiting helplessly to be blasted out of the sea. As they drew near Captain Ryan ordered:

"Pat to TF: Open fire with any caliber that will bear."

That was the signal for the slaughter. For once the *O'Bannon* was a Goliath instead of a David. Every five-inch and 20-mm. on her decks opened up. Her first target was a motor-driven barge, large as an LCI. Shells walked, then leaped on her. She jumped out of the water, no longer a solid, black mass, but a bouncing orange ball of fire that rolled on the sea.

The *Nicholas* engaged two small barges that vanished abruptly. The officers on the *O'Bannon's* bridge were silent. But this was war, and the troops and ammunition out there in the blackness were meant to claim American lives. The annihilation went on. Some barges were filled with gasoline. When hit they mounted high into dull red columns, broad at the base and spraying the sea with liquid fire.

When all were burning, some completely disintegrated after a few minutes, the TBS called:

"Pat to TF: Illuminate the beach and see if any are hiding over there."

The *O'Bannon* and the *Chevalier* fired a number of flares

about the beach and caught two more barges lurking in the shadows.

"Get them, Bill," MacDonald shouted, and salvos pinned the barges to the shoreline, blasting them into splintered bits of wood.

At Captain Ryan's command the ships joined up to retire. Ten minutes later Jap planes swooped down over the formation and selected the *O'Bannon* as their target. Lieutenant Burford's secondary battery of 20-mm.'s began chattering and tracers flew about the diving Japs.

The Japs refused to be stopped. Swooping down amidst the red and white tracers, they dropped several sticks of bombs off the *O'Bannon's* port quarter and starboard bow.

In the fireroom bulbs burst in their sockets and dirt and chips of cork flew about the men. Repair parties ran through the ship, inspecting every bulkhead, but no damage had been done.

The planes refused to attack again but darted about the speeding column boxing it with flares. After twenty minutes of zooming and diving over the foremasts of the ships, they turned away to head for their base.

One of Zimmerman's firemen who had been topside came hurrying down the ladder. During the salvo fire he had been knocked flat by the concussion of one of the guns.

"Never again," he told Zimmerman. "You can get killed up there, Zip, why even the damn breeze knocks you down." He kept shaking his head.

"No more for me. I'll stay down here where it's nice and safe."

Zimmerman grinned. He remembered the night the *O'Bannon* had had her first taste of depth charges and this same boy, frightened and almost weeping, had left his battle station and attempted to scramble up the fireroom ladder.

It seemed a long time ago.

14 VELLA LAVELLA

THE PERIOD OF night evacuation of Kolombangara by the Japs had begun. Under cover of darkness barges laden with Jap troops sneaked up the Slot. Night after night the *O'Bannon* and her sister ships intercepted and destroyed them. The Japs tried to protect their barges with heavy air cover, and nightly fifty to a hundred bombs dropped around the ships. Miraculously none was hit.

As days passed the sweeps became longer. The ships would leave Tulagi at noon and completely circle Vella Lavella searching out barges found hugging the protection of the shores and blasting them to splintered wood. The ghastly toll of enemy troops mounted higher and higher. Not a night went by that Jap planes—sometimes as many as ten at a time—did not attack. The hours at General Quarters became longer and left exhausted men and officers wondering how long it would last and how it would end.

September slipped into October. As the days went on the officers and crew of the *O'Bannon* began to accept the sounds of their ship daily preparing for battle as commonplace, just as a man who works in a noisy office comes to accept its sounds as part of his daily environment.

The fear that death might be their shipmate any night, the drudging ordeal, the confinement, the tension, the oppressive feeling from watching scurrying barges loaded down with men and deserted by their navy being blasted to flaming death, all assumed the proportions of a horrible normality.

The men were listless. Officers and crew alike had lost much weight. Captain MacDonald found his clothes hung on his body like a badly fitted suit; the thin aquiline nose of Lieutenant Pfeifer seemed more pointed; Ensign Creigh had grown more silent; even Ensign "Slim Jim" Garten forgot to talk of his feud with Hollywood and looked like a thin, adolescent boy as he moved about the bridge.

To talk in more than monosyllables was an effort. Meals in the wardroom would open with a bustle of conversation, only to die away in complete silence before they finished.

Acute sense of time and space was benumbed. The only thing real was the ship, the commands, the sun scorching like a branding iron—and the sea, always motionless and reflecting the white-hot glare.

Death, heretofore a taboo subject, was openly discussed. It was abruptly brought out in the open. One night a group of the crew was lounging on the fantail playing with Peggy. Her one leg was still slightly stiff, and as she hobbled about it gave her a laughable, clownish gait. Tired of pleading for bits of chocolate, she lay back in the lap of her owner, who moved his hand slowly up and down her back as he joined in the conversation.

Suddenly one of the firemen, a short, chubby boy who had been discussing the merits of a girl in Sydney by the name of Sal, spoke during a lull in the talk:

"You know guys, I wonder what happens when you're dead."

Startled at his own words, he immediately added:

"Honest, I'm not kidding, I've been thinking about it since the night the *Strong* got bumped. I wonder is it nice and peaceful like they say."

Once started, the discussion grew. The talk jumped from one boy to another as if it were a rubber ball bouncing in a circle. One boy insisted, "I'm willing to take a chance of getting killed if it means getting some peace."

Another boy agreed, putting his hands inside the belt of his dungarees to show how much weight he had lost, saying, "How the hell long do you think it's going to go on? Christ, they've got to relieve us sometime, don't they?"

A boy answered, "Replace, not relieve, buddy."

The next day the phrase spread throughout the ship. It became a grim motto, said as a jest by boys who stared death in the face and felt no fear. Increasingly, cases of physical and nervous exhaustion came into Dr. Manchester's sick bay. It wasn't unusual for him to hear, "I can't sleep, Doc, I feel as if I'm smothering in my bunk. I can't breathe and I break out in cold sweats."

Or a man would drop his tools and suddenly go to his bunk biting his lips and squeezing back tears that seemed to come from deep within.

On the afternoon of October 5 the *O'Bannon*, *Selfridge*, and *Chevalier* made a large sweep, dipping deep into Kula Gulf. Visibility was good, but nothing was sighted and the ships swung about to return to Tulagi Anchorage. Just off the Russell Islands flags fluttered up and down the *Selfridge's* hoist. It was a message from Admiral Wilkinson.

"Return up the Slot, speed of twenty knots. More later. Prepare to execute turn. Execute turn."

The three destroyers made a complete circle to steam back toward Kula Gulf. In the *O'Bannon's* pilothouse officers looked questioningly at Captain MacDonald. What had happened? Why were the ships returning? The answer came at once.

Ensign "Slim Jim" Garten on the decoding watch walked into the pilothouse. His face was pale under his deep tan. He seemed stunned. In his hand he held a message upside down. His voice was hoarse.

"Message, Captain."

"Thanks, Jim," MacDonald said and read the message. He looked up.

"Information has been received, gentlemen, that there is a force of nine destroyers, cruisers, PT boats, and SC's (sub chasers), headed our way. It looks as if the Japs will really make a stand tonight to evacuate their troops from Vella Lavella. They have been sighted off Choiseul. The Admiral has ordered Commander H. O. Larson and three destroyers to join us at ten miles west of Sauka Point. We will probably meet them at 2330."

He turned to Lieutenant Pfeifer:

"We can take time out going up, Carl. The Admiral wants twenty knots. Sound General Quarters at 2000."

Word spread throughout the ship that a large task force was to be engaged that night. Crew members gathered in small knots to discuss the report.

"Maybe we'll get a hit tonight and get some damage and Cianca can go back to school," one said. Usually everybody grinned at the Brooklyn boy, for it was an old joke how some of the chiefs threatened to call the nearest truant officer when they thought Cianca was paying too much attention to one spot of rust he was chipping and painting. But this time there were no smiles.

Tonight, they felt, something was going to happen. They had waited for it a long time. They knew that sometime their luck would give out. By the law of averages it must be tonight.

When he heard the contents of the message Chief Padgett turned to his friend Guess:

"Well, George, we're outnumbered three to one. Looks like tonight is the night." He held out his hand. "It was nice knowing you, fellow."

Guess gripped the outstretched hand. He stood up and picked two life jackets from a shelf.

"Don't forget, Pat, about those letters."

Padgett nodded. Both men wriggled into the jackets.

In the fireroom, Zimmerman and Unroe went from man to man offering words of encouragement, giving last minute instructions, making tests of gauges and dials, and handing out life jackets.

The two Conklin brothers, separated in the aft and firerooms, came up to Zimmerman and asked, "Chief, can you put us together tonight just in case something happens?"

After a conference with Engineering Officer Bates, Zimmerman put both boys working side by side.

All day the ships steamed slowly toward Kula Gulf. Under the relentless sun, the motionless sea stretched like a sheet of green glass merging with the thin line of the horizon.

The sunset was blood-red, and night followed quickly. A bright moon rose and the sea moved with a long, languid swell. Shortly after darkness settled about the ships MacDonald addressed his men. His talk was simple, almost to the point of briskness:

"Men, this is your captain," he said. "Tonight we have information of enemy activity consisting of enemy barges and destroyers. We are going to meet them. General Quarters will be sounded at 2000. Wear your life jackets—it may be a cold night. Take plenty of water to your battle stations. It will be a long night. That is all."

The loudspeaker snapped off and the men settled down for the action they were to see. In spite of the sticky heat their life jackets gave them a sense of comfort—just in case.

General Quarters was sounded. The force moved nearer to Vella Lavella. The TBS speaker had been silent. Officers took their positions on the bridge, nervously tightening a knot on life jackets or playing with binoculars hanging from their necks on lanyards.

At 2030 the lookout called, "Planes approaching. . . . They are enemy planes."

Now they could hear the droning of the Japs circling over the ships. Flares were dropped, marking their course. But there was no whistling of falling bombs, just the dazzling lights of the flares, dangling beneath the small paper parachutes.

"They want to know exactly where we are tonight," MacDonald said, turning to Lieutenant Pfeifer. "It looks like they're leading us into something."

Blinker lights flashed on the *Selfridge*.

"Commander Larson will not be able to rendezvous until 0100," the message read.

The three destroyers now stood alone against the powerful Jap task force.

The *Chevalier* called the *Selfridge:*

"Kitty to John: We have contact, bearing two-seven-oh."

Finally the lookouts called, "Bridge. Two groups of ships."

The officers stiffened. Except for their heavy breathing complete silence hung about the dim pilothouse.

Someone said, "This is it." And a voice answered, "You're not kidding."

Now the TBS was alive with code calls.

"Kitty to Mary: I have contact. Looks like five cans."

"Mary to Kitty: I have them. Some more stuff, too."

"Kitty to John: Can you make them out?"

"John to Kitty: No, not yet."

"Kitty to John: Wait until they come closer."

The lookout shouted, "Bridge. Two groups."

The flagship ordered: "John to TF: Close for attack. Follow me."

The two lines of Jap ships had separated to cross the bow of the *Chevalier*, leading the line. Admiral Wilkinson's force, between the Jap columns, charged straight ahead.

Through his glasses MacDonald could see the Jap formation on the *O'Bannon's* starboard side. It consisted of five ships with a Ubari-class cruiser, long and low in the water, the inverted "Y" stack spilling aft. He selected the cruiser as his target. He turned to Lieutenant Pfeifer:

"Carl, we'll fire first with torpedoes, then engage with gunfire."

"Aye, aye, Captain," his executive officer answered.

Then turning to Mitchell on the starboard bridge wing, MacDonald called,

"Fire torpedoes to starboard, Mitch. Let me know when ready."

The *Chevalier* moved closer to the Jap line. The *Selfridge* and *O'Bannon* followed. The ships drew closer across the moon-splashed water. It appeared both Jap columns were maneuvering to hem Admiral Wilkinson's force within a giant "V."

Suddenly the TBS barked:

"John to TF: Fire torpedoes," and MacDonald ordered his torpedo officer: "Fire when ready."

Almost immediately Mitchell snapped:

147

"Fire one . . . fire two . . . fire three . . . fire four . . . fire five . . . fire six . . .

"Half salvo expended, sir."

The *O'Bannon* and her sister ships still bore in. At MacDonald's command the *O'Bannon's* five-inch rifles began seeking out the Jap cruiser. After the first few salvos a flame shot up from her midships. It grew higher, licking about the superstructure.

In the meantime the *Selfridge* had engaged the leading Jap destroyer in a gun duel. From the bridge of the *O'Bannon* the men could see the Jap lurch out of line, flames running across her decks.

A third Jap ship was dead in the water, and the *Chevalier's* guns ripped its steel body to pieces. It was soon a burning hulk.

The other Jap column swung about and started to flee before completing its run. Then a third Jap column was reported by the lookout, north of the first two lines of Jap ships, but this too was turning away.

One destroyer of the first Jap column held its ground, its gun flashes lighting up the night. The *Chevalier* charged at the ship, every one of her guns roaring in continuous fire.

Shells exploded on the superstructure of the Jap and she fled.

The cruiser hit by the *O'Bannon* was now about 6,000 yards off her bow burning fiercely. Through their glasses the officers watched her. Explosion after explosion rumbled across the sea. Then suddenly the ship disappeared in an eruption of flame and burning wreckage hurled more than 500 feet by a monster blast that shook the night for miles around. Bits of fiery metal rained over the sea, and in a few minutes the flames vanished abruptly, like an extinguished candle.

The destruction of the Jap cruiser was so complete that not even a flaming hull was left to slide under the surface of the sea.

Lieutenant Pfeifer whistled and looked at Captain MacDonald. "That was the worst I've ever seen, Captain," he said.

MacDonald lowered his glasses.

"We must have hit her magazine, George," he said. "It was the most terrific explosion I've ever had the pleasure of seeing on a Jap ship. Let's get some more." He asked Simmons, "Have you a solution, Bill?"

"Aye, aye, Captain," the gunnery officer answered.

"Resume fire."

The *O'Bannon's* guns selected a Jap destroyer. It too held its ground and answered salvo for salvo. Shells burst off the *O'Bannon's* stern and the men topside could hear them moan through the air. The *Chevalier, Selfridge,* and the *O'Bannon* now stood in line. The flashes of their guns were dull red through billows of smoke. Three Jap ships were now burning.

Suddenly MacDonald saw a burst of flame rise from the *Chevalier's* portside. A torpedo had ripped through her side, splitting her in half. The entire ship separated as if a giant knife had sliced her in two. The stern turned about and swung into the path of the *O'Bannon.*

"Hard right rudder," MacDonald screamed. The helmsman swung the wheel violently, and the *O'Bannon* lay on her side as she answered her rudder, but the charging stern of the *Chevalier,* as if steered by a phantom quartermaster, also swung about and into the *O'Bannon's* path. The ships must collide.

"Back emergency," MacDonald shouted, and the helmsman grabbed the fireroom annunciators, pulling back the handles violently, shouting, "Emergency."

The *O'Bannon* reared, her stern deep, like a high-spirited horse pulled up short by the bit. She gripped the sea, but her fierce momentum kept shoving her forward.

"Stand by for a ram . . . stand by for a ram."

Every officer on the bridge grabbed the small brass rail running around the pilothouse. Crew members lunged for metal supports, gun mounts. In the fireroom men who might be trapped in an inferno of scalding steam dropped their tools and held onto railings and ladders, their faces tight with apprehension. In the handling room and magazine, men threw themselves on the deck, eyeing the stacks of shells and tins of powder.

In a few seconds the *O'Bannon* hit the *Chevalier.* Metal crunched against metal, then the ships bounced clear. The luck of the *O'Bannon* still held. It was a glancing blow that bit into the *Chevalier's* after engine room.

The *Chevalier* lay dead in the water, a gaping hole in her starboard side, while the beautiful bow of the *O'Bannon* was a mass of twisted metal bent back more than twenty-five feet.

While both ships lay still in the water, the gallant little *Selfridge* charged alone at four fleeing Jap ships firing over their shoulders. Jap planes joined in the attack and flares lighted the night. The *Selfridge* had scored one hit on a destroyer when suddenly she received a torpedo hit which tore her in two.

Mitchell shouted: "*Selfridge* hit, Captain."

MacDonald grabbed his glasses and through them he could see the flame-engulfed destroyer circling slowly.

Two of the fleeing Jap ships turned around and began laying a heavy smoke screen around one of their crippled destroyers. MacDonald shouted, "Bill, get on those two targets."

"Aye, aye, Captain," Simmons answered.

"Commence firing, director," MacDonald ordered.

Salvos arched over the *Chevalier* to the circling destroyers, which immediately left their ship burning helplessly in the thick, half-completed smoke screen.

Aboard the *Chevalier* a light blinked: "We are sinking. Please assist us."

MacDonald turned to Lieutenant Pfeifer: "Send Repair One to see what damage we have."

Word was passed swiftly to Chief Boatswain Picton, "Captain wants to know damage forward."

"Okay, gang," the chief told his men loaded down with shoring. His gang of seven poured down the forward fireroom hatch, down still another ladder, until they were two decks below in a dim world of cables, steel supports, lighted only by the electric hand lanterns they carried. But each man knew every foot of the darkness. They had been over this part of the ship hundreds of times in practice drills, carrying planks of wood, acetylene torches, saws, chisels, and hammers—they moved, sometimes on hands and knees, far to the bow of the ship. Water splashed over their feet, and then they saw the *O'Bannon's* injury—a deep ten-foot gash. The bow had been sheared off until it resembled a jagged saw. The blow had carried away the anchor-chain room, the boatswain supply room, and the paint locker. A ripple extended along the deck as far aft as Number One gun mount, from the keel to topside. Slabs of timber were slapped against the hole and braced with beams against the opposite bulkhead. The men worked furiously in the dim light of their lanterns.

The light on the *Chevalier* was blinking again:

"We are going fast. I am dead in the water."

On the bridge MacDonald was receiving reports from Bates in the engine room. The crash, he said, had not injured the electrical or engineering plants. It was in the pilothouse that the *O'Bannon's* injury was felt. The ship couldn't answer her rudder. MacDonald barked orders to the helmsman. The ship jerked and shuddered as the quartermaster spun the wheel to port or starboard.

He finally maneuvered the *O'Bannon* to within forty yards of the *Chevalier*.

"We can't get any closer," MacDonald snapped to Lieutenant Pfeifer. "Signal the *Chevalier* that we are sending our boats over to pick his men up."

The order had just left his lips when three Jap bombers zoomed down and released a stick of bombs. They exploded with a roar off the *O'Bannon's* stern and sent sheets of water high in the air.

More bombs dropped, followed by showers of flares. Against the backdrop of harsh white light the *Chevalier* settled rapidly. Boats were being lowered off the *O'Bannon* and the screech of protesting davits could be heard plainly. Less than 6,000 yards ahead a Jap destroyer was still burning. Then the lookout reported:

"Bridge. Group of ships coming toward us. 12,000 yards."

The silence in the pilothouse was electric. Padgett's voice again: "It looks like five."

MacDonald's order was quiet. "Bill, stand by."

Suddenly the TBS coughed:

"Fox to John: We will pick up enemy ships and *Selfridge*."

A sigh went up from the officers. The approaching ships were Lieutenant Commander Larson's supporting destroyer squadron which had been ordered to rendezvous with them earlier in the evening by Admiral Wilkinson.

Burning flares still floated on the sea. MacDonald hurried to the wings of the bridge. He could see the wakes of the whaleboats as they moved through the water. The sea was alive with swimming men. It looked like a school of porpoises. The crew of the abandoned *Chevalier* had jumped into the sea.

"All hands who can swim, over the side," MacDonald shouted. The *O'Bannon's* crew needed no second order. Men flung themselves over the lifeline. Above the splashes and the bellowing commands of the chiefs on deck, MacDonald heard a strange sound. It was singing. He lifted his binoculars and through them he saw a group of boys, hands locked together, in a circle holding up injured shipmates, moving toward the *O'Bannon*. They were singing—almost shouting—at the top of their voices, "California, Here We Come."

Survivors were now reaching the *O'Bannon's* decks. One of the first crew members of the *Chevalier* to reach the lowered cargo net off the *O'Bannon's* side was a young boy pushing a tin can. A line was flung to him. Treading water, he calmly began to tie the rope about the can. A chief on deck screamed:

"Goddammit grab that line. What the hell are you doing?"

The boy shouted, "Take it easy, Chief, these are my tailored blues. What the hell do you think I brought them over here for?" He finished tying the can and yelled, "Okay, hoist it up." The amazed chief pulled it aboard. Then the boy scrambled up the net.

The first of the *Chevalier's* survivors brought aboard were coated with thick oil. They fell on the deck retching and gagging. Crew members lifted them onto stretchers and raced to the wardroom, which Dr. Manchester and his pharmacist's mates had turned into an emergency hospital.

Men were laid gently on tables. Some screamed as layers of burned flesh fell in strips from their bodies. Most were silent. A few moaned and cried. Some had deep gashes on their bodies, and blood rolled off their dungarees to mix with the inch-thick coat of oil on the deck of the officers' country. Others brought in were examined briefly by Dr. Manchester. They lay limp on the cots as he ripped aside a shirt and listened for a heartbeat.

"Take this man out to the fantail," he would say shortly. "He is dead."

Under the direction of Pharmacist's Mate Second Class Allen Harper, boatload after boatload was rushed in to Manchester, who worked steadily, washing wounds, whispering a word of comfort to a boy he knew must die before dawn, or snapping orders to Chief Pharmacist's Mate James McCook. On the *O'Bannon's* quarterdeck, Finnell treated minor cuts and gashes.

The line of stretchers brought in by Rowland's messmen never seemed to end. One boy lying in a thick pool of his own blood tried to struggle to his feet as Manchester bent over him. His arms had been blown off at the shoulder.

"Doc," he whispered. Then he fell back. His eyes closed. Manchester shook his head. "Too late," he said.

One messman, tears rolling down his brown cheeks, sobbed:

"God damn those Jap bastards . . . God damn them to hell . . ." as he pulled a blanket over the boy's face.

On deck, Smith, the boy who never forgot to take his daily exercise with the dumbbells, heard a shout—"I can't make it . . . I can't make it . . . help me." Fifty feet from the *O'Bannon* a man splashed feebly in the water. Smith dove over the side. In a few minutes he was beside the man, saying, "Take it easy, buddy, I'll take over now."

The man was a dead weight in his arms. Smith held onto him with one hand and swam hard through the swells. He reached the net and with one hand grabbed the rope and struggled upward, inch by inch, his breath coming in long, sobbing gasps. On deck he lifted the sailor in his arms and stumbled to the wardroom.

"Doc," he panted, "this guy is hurt bad." Manchester, bending over a boy on a cot, looked up and pushed through the crowded room. Opening his eyes, the sailor looked up at Smith and grinned:

"I swam away from that one okay, now I can see the wife and kids." He sighed and closed his eyes. His body, cradled in Smith's arms, seemed to slump like a broken sack of flour.

Manchester reached Smith's side and ripped open the oil-drenched shirt. He listened for a heartbeat, he pushed back an eyelid, and then felt the man's arms and body.

"Sorry, Smith," he said, "he's dead. It's a miracle he got this far. There's not a bone left whole in his body. Crushed to jelly by the concussion."

Smith slowly picked up the still body. He walked back on deck to the fantail, where a strip of canvas covered six other dead men. He quietly put the body of the sailor down, folded the arms across the chest and pulled back the canvas shroud.

"I'm sorry, buddy," he said quietly. "I did my best."

In the wardroom Captain Wilson of the *Chevalier*, his leg badly shattered, was brought in to Manchester.

"Never mind me, Doc," he said, "take care of the kids first."

While Manchester and his pharmacist's mates gave blood plasma, dressed wounds, and set broken bones, Captain Wilson spoke words of encouragement to his men. He picked out boy after boy, saying,

"Take it easy now, this old Dr. Manchester is the best saw-bones in the Navy."

Every officer's bunk had been turned over to the injured. In MacDonald's quarters lay a boy with broken legs and arms.

On the bridge MacDonald and his officers were in constant communication with the men deep in the damaged bow. Finally Lieutenant Pfeifer, ordered by MacDonald to rescue operations, reported that 85 per cent of the *Chevalier's* personnel had been rescued and no more were to be found. It was only then that MacDonald said,

"We can't do any more here. Let's head for home. Pass the word to the repair party that we will go one-third speed. Let me have a report on how the bulkheads hold." Then he ordered the quartermaster:

"All ahead one-third."

The ship shuddered as the screws bit savagely in the sea. Picton reported, "She's holding."

MacDonald sighed wearily. He turned to Lieutenant Pfeifer, "Looks like we'll make it. Take over, I'm going to see how Captain Wilson is."

Down in the wardroom Dr. Manchester looked up at his captain's entrance.

"We have twenty-four down here, Captain. I have life jackets for all if anything happens."

MacDonald walked over to the injured captain of the *Chevalier* and sat at the edge of his bunk.

"I'm sorry this had to happen, George."

Captain Wilson smiled. His hair was thick with oil that kept rolling down his cheeks in tiny rivulets.

"We'll get another crack at them, Mac," he said.

On his way back to the bridge Captain MacDonald noticed a young officer limping on the deck talking to some of the survivors. As he came closer MacDonald recognized Lieutenant Hanson, the *Chevalier's* executive officer.

"Are you hurt, old chap?" he asked. The officer shook his head, "Just a little bump, Captain." But at MacDonald's insistence he went to the wardroom to be examined. Later it was reported that the "little bump" was a leg fractured in two places.

The night was tar-black. Even the stars were hidden. Sudden squalls swept the decks, washing away the blood and oil. Toward early morning Jap planes were reported, but a squall appeared and the *O'Bannon* disappeared in the friendly shelter of the driving downpour.

The decks were crowded with the oil-covered survivors. Uninjured, but stunned by the shock of the sinking, they refused to go below. When the rain slashed across the ship they huddled in small groups, seeking the shelter of the rafts on the weather decks, of the torpedo tubes, and even the spud lockers.

One boy, still groggy from the blast, spotted the spread of canvas on the fantail under which some of his shipmates lay. He crept under its shelter.

All night the *O'Bannon*, with her cargo of dead and injured men, moved through the rainy blackness. With every burst of speed she shuddered, her engines faithfully trying to obey the commands of her bridge. Once, after the helmsman desperately swung the wheel without any answer from the rudder, one officer said softly, "She can't help it. She's hurt bad."

It was late afternoon when the *O'Bannon* limped into Tulagi. On deck messmen were shouting:

"Coffee for survivors in the crew's quarters . . . get it while it's hot . . ."

The boy who had been sleeping under the canvas covering on the fantail stood up and stretched. He nudged one of the silent figures.

"Come on," he growled, "let's get some Joe."

There was no answer. He called again. One of the *O'Bannon's* chiefs walked over and took his arm.

"Never mind them, kid, they're beyond coffee." The boy looked up, startled: "What do you mean, Chief?"

"They're dead, kid," was the answer. The boy's eyes became big, and the blood drained from his face. "Christ," he whispered, "I've been asking one of the guys all night why the hell he was so cold."

15 HOME

WITH THE *CHEVALIER'S* dead and injured removed to the hospital at Tulagi, the *O'Bannon's* crew set about cleaning their ship. Blood and oil were everywhere. Weary, exhausted men, still shocked from the scenes they had witnessed only a few hours before, mopped and swabbed the decks and officers' country.

It was the next day before naval inspectors arrived to examine the damaged bow. The decision was, "Temporary repairs until you reach Mare Island."

Just before dark, Captain MacDonald announced to his crew: "Men, this is your captain. I have just received word that we are to proceed, as soon as temporary repairs have been made, to the West Coast." He added simply: "We are going home."

A few days later, the *O'Bannon* limped out of Tulagi, her bow a patchwork of steel plates, bound for the United States. Her turbines seemed to sing: ". . . Home. . . . Home. . . . Home."

That night, to Lieutenant Pfeifer, who was walking along the weather deck on a routine inspection, the ship seemed to wear an uncertain and restless air. He noticed how crew members, leaning or sitting against a bulkhead, would walk over to the lifeline, gaze out into the impenetrable blackness, then return to their original position. Gunner's mates would open the steel doors of their mounts, peep in, then slam them shut. On the bridge some of the officers would step into the sound room and listen to the eternal pinging of Soundman Conn's equipment.

After several minutes they would leave, scowling at the sound gear as if they had been disappointed because its radiating waves had failed to locate a submarine.

In the fireroom, Unroe grumbled to one of his watertenders: "I don't know what the hell is wrong with me. I keep thinking we're headed up the Slot."

And little Finley, who had no more battles to describe, walked about the ship like a lost soul.

In his cabin, Captain MacDonald tossed and turned until finally he was forced to dress and return to the breeze.

"Just getting a breath of air," he volunteered as he sat on the port bridge wing. Once he had to shake himself when he caught himself wondering when he would hear the cry of "Bridge. Contact," followed by the general-quarters alarm, the hurried pounding of feet across the steel deck, turrets slamming, and Bess's clear voice chanting the range. That was over. With each turn of her turbines the *O'Bannon* was taking them away from all that. Somehow this fact seemed hard to accept.

As he passed the forward fireroom hatch, Lieutenant Pfeifer saw one of the Conklin brothers climbing on deck. He was holding some letter paper, and a fountain pen was clenched in his teeth. With his semi-nakedness still glistening with the heat of the fireroom, the boy reminded Pfeifer of a pirate boarding a ship with a knife between his jaws. He chuckled at the comparison, and the boy—it was "young" Conklin—grinned up at him.

"Don't seem right not meeting any Japs tonight, Mr. Pfeifer," the boy said as he passed.

"You're certainly right," the officer answered.

The next day toward early afternoon, most of the chiefs were gathered in their quarters. Some were sipping coffee listening to Spracklin, while others sat around in the warm breeze blowing down the hatchway, reading, writing letters, or playing cards. Suddenly a crew member dropped the heavy hatch cover he had been repairing. It fell with a tremendous crash. The CPO's leaped to their feet, coffee jugs, letters flying about as they scrambled to the deck.

In the warm sunshine topside they accepted the apologies of the crew member. Back in their quarters someone said:

"Sounded like a damn bomb to me." Everybody nodded but nobody laughed.

Two weeks later the *O'Bannon* steamed into the Golden Gate. As the destroyer neared Mare Island, Captain MacDonald stepped out on one of the bridge wings and let his eyes take in the long, slim length of his ship.

Like her crew, she was battle-worn, but she still retained the graceful lines that first caught the admiration of Gunner's Mate Spracklin as she lay at her dock in Bath sixteen long months before.

It was only on closer inspection that you could see that the thin dangerous bow was twisted; the decks worn smooth by countless footsteps, and the steel showing at the muzzles of her guns, where the paint had been eaten away by salvos that had ripped the Japanese Imperial Fleet from Guadalcanal to Vella Lavella. Besides, the tops of her stacks were smudged by soot, her lines stiff with salt, her hull weather-beaten by the flying spray.

Her crew too had changed. The 100,000 or more miles the *O'Bannon* had traveled in battle, and the countless day-and-night vigils at battle stations had taken their toll on the boys MacDonald could see eagerly lining the lifeline. Boys who had innocently asked their chief "where is the front of the boat?" were now veterans of numerous major sea engagements. Their eyes were hard, and they laughed suddenly in high-pitched voices at trivial things. The drop of a dish was enough to send them bouncing to their feet, nerves taut as a C-string.

Her young officers had aged considerably. All had lost weight. Some had a touch of gray in their hair, while Captain MacDonald's curly black hair was completely silver.

It was noon when the *O'Bannon* moved into Mare Island. Lines were cast and she was made fast.

On the bridge Captain MacDonald kept saying over and over to himself in quiet disbelief:

"It's all over . . ."

He walked back to his emergency cabin to finish packing.

He picked up the picture of the girl named Cecilia and looked at it in silence, then digging deep in his breast pocket he held the St. Christopher's medal in his hand.

"Thank you, O merciful God," he whispered.

On deck, stacks of mail had been brought aboard, and boys stood about reading one letter with three or more tucked in a blouse. Louis Cianca tore one open that had an official look to it.

He read it once, then roared. It was a notice asking him to explain his absence from his classrooms in the Alexander Hamilton High School, Brooklyn, and to please report at once.

He picked up his seabag and told a grinning shipmate as they moved to the gangway:

"If I'm late getting back to the ship, I got a good excuse. I'll just tell Captain Mac I was kept in after school!"

The U.S.S. *O'Bannon* was home.
There wasn't a Purple Heart on board.

THE SECRETARY OF THE NAVY

WASHINGTON

The President of the United States takes pleasure in presenting the PRESIDENTIAL UNIT CITATION to the

UNITED STATES SHIP O'BANNON

for service as set forth in the following

· CITATION:

"For outstanding performance in combat against enemy Japanese forces in the South Pacific from October 7, 1942, to October 7, 1943. An aggressive veteran after a year of continuous and intensive operations in this area, the U.S.S. O'BANNON has taken tremendous toll of vital Japanese warships, surface vessels and aircraft. Launching a close range attack on hostile combatant ships off Guadalcanal on the night of November 13, 1942, the O'BANNON scored three torpedo hits on a Japanese battleship, boldly engaged two other men o'war with gunfire and retired safely in spite of damage sustained. During three days of incessant hostilities in July 1943, she gallantly stood down Kula Gulf to bombard enemy shore positions in coverage of our assault groups, later taking a valiant part in the rescue of survivors from the torpedoed U.S.S. STRONG while under fierce coastal battery fire and aerial bombing attack and adding her fire power toward the destruction of a large Japanese naval force. In company with two destroyers, the O'BANNON boldly intercepted and repulsed nine hostile warships off Vella Lavella on October 7, 1943, destroying two enemy ships and damaging others. Although severely damaged, she stood by to take aboard and care for survivors of a friendly torpedoed destroyer and retired to base under her own power. The O'BANNON's splendid achievements and the gallant fighting spirit of her officers and men reflect great credit upon the United States Naval Service."

For the President,

Frank Knox

Secretary of the Navy

The Officers and Men of the U.S.S. *O'Bannon*

With Their Present Ranks and Ratings

Capt. Edwin R. Wilkinson, USN,
North Miami, Fla.

Capt. Harold F. Pullen, USN,
Melrose, Mass.

Capt. Alvin D. Chandler, USN,
Williamsburg, Va.

Cdr. Donald J. MacDonald, USN,
New York, N. Y.

Cdr. George Philip, Jr., USN,
Rapid City, S. D.

Lt. Carl F. Pfeifer, USN,
Springfield, Ohio.

Lt. Cdr. Robert C. Manchester,
(MC), USNR,
Alliance, Ohio.

Lt. Cdr. Richard M. Rowe, USNR,
Memphis, Tenn.

Lt. David S. Wilson, USN,
Hampden-Sydney, Va.

Lt. Lanson B. Ditto, Jr., USNR,
Paducah, Ky.

Lt. Edwin H. Kiefer, USNR,
Hollywood, Calif.

Lt. Malcolm M. Dunham, (MC),
USNR,
Woodbridge, N. J.

Lt. Doral B. Eardley, USNR,
Salt Lake City, Utah.

Lt. Ray Thomas, USNR,
Galveston, Texas.

Lt. John D. Creigh, USNR,
Chicago, Ill.

Lt. Douglas P. Bates, USNR,
Baton Rouge, La.

Lt. Lendall B. Knight, USNR,
Alfred, Maine.

Lt. Harry P. Burford, USNR,
Los Angeles, Calif.

Lt. William E. Simmons, USN,
Jenkintown, Pa.

Lt. James R. Garten, USNR,
Odon, Indiana.

Lt. John P. Tazewell, USN,
Norfolk, Va.

Lt. (jg) Dennis M. Mitchell, USNR,
Wilmette, Ill.

Lt. (jg) John J. Noonan, Jr., USNR,
Richmond, Va.

Lt. Daniel L. Martin, USNR,
St. Petersburg, Fla.

Lt. (jg) Arthur O. Huck, USNR,
Darien, Conn.

Lt. (jg) George H. Freetage, USNR,
Sebring, Ohio.

Lt. (jg) Edward C. Schwartz, USNR,
Evansville, Ind.

Lt. (jg) Thomas T. Murphy, USNR,
Brookline, Mass.

Lt. (jg) Richard L. Knox, USNR,
Minneapolis, Minn.

Lt. (jg) Joseph M. Coccellato,
USNR,
San Francisco, Calif.

Lt. Bob J. McGrath, USN,
El Cerrito, Calif.

Lt. (jg) John T. Sexton, USN,
Stratford, Conn.

Lt. (jg) Irvin R. Fahrbach, USN,
Menasha, Wisc.

Ch Pay Clk Mack Huggins, USN,
Norfolk, Va.

Adams, George, Cox, USN
Kearny, N. J.

Adkison, Ralph A., RdM3c(T) USN
Akron, O.

Alcorn, Robert J., F2c, USNR
San Diego, Calif.

Alexander, Richard W., S1c, USNR
Muncie, Ind.

Alloway, John W., Jr., Cox, USN
Etowah, Tenn.

Anderson, Bernard C., CPhM(AA),
USN
South Gate, Calif.

Anderson, William L., S1c, USNR
Galesburg, Ill.

Archer, Edmund C., SC3c, USN
Brooklyn, N. Y.

Armstrong, Lynn H., FC2c (T),
USN
Portland, Ore.

Armstrong, Oliver D., StM2c, USNR
Shreveport, La.

Artesani, John H., SoM3c, USNR
Brighton, Mass.

Arthur, Robert C., SK2c, USNR
Waterloo, Ia.

Atkinson, Howard C., CMoMM
(RAT), USN
Blackwell, Okla.

Ball, Joseph L., FCR2c(T), USNR
Hewett, W. Va.

Bartosh, Don (n), S1c, USNR
Texas City, Tex.

Baxendale, Albert E., FC2c(M), USN
Irwin, Pa.

Bayles, Harry Elwood, Cox, USNR
Dover, N. J.

Beers, Manley H., S1c, USNR
Northport, N. Y.

Bernad, Joseph A., GM1c, USNR
East Landsdowne, Pa.

Bess, James O., Ensign (T), USN
Napa, Calif.

Biesucci, Raphael, S1c, USNR
East Rutherford, N. J.

Biloon, Ralph J., SoM3c, USNR
Wilmington, Del.

Blair, William E., Cox (T), USN
Broken Arrow, Okla.

Bohacs, John J., GM3c, USNR
Carteret, N. J.

Bowman, William E., Chief Radioman (T)
Winthrop, Mass.

Boyte, George O., RM3c, USNR
Washington, D. C.

Brandt, Lucas M., TM2c, USNR
Gardiner, Mont.

Braun, Ulrich J., CTM, USN
Newport, R. I.

Breininger, Robert W., WT1c, USN
Battle Creek, Mich.

Brennan, Richard P., S1c, USN
Brooklyn, N. Y.

Brighenti, William J., S1c, USNR
Lee, Mass.

Brittain, Robert P., MM1c, USNR
Newton, Kan.

Brodeur, Joseph R., Jr., CGM(AA),
USN
Augusta, Ga.

Brown, Brooks (n) MoMM3c, USN
Andalusia, Ala.

Brown, Daniel Moses, CQM(AA)
(T), USN
St. Louis, Mo.

Brown, Robert J., TM2c, USNR
Erie, Pa.

Buboltz, Stanley J., RDM3c, USNR
Kingston, N. J.

Burcham, Robert C., SoM3c, USNR
Wilmington, Del.

Butler, Bob G., RM3c, USNR
Tulsa, Okla.

Butterfield, Wyartt B., S1c, USN
Trenton, N. J.

Bykerk, George M., GM3c, USN
Lincoln, Nebr.

Byrd, Francis H., WT1c, USN
San Leandro, Calif.

Cain, Sylvester M., Jr., MM1c, USNR
Moberly, Mo.

Carll, Benjamin F., S1c, USN
Bellerose, N. Y.

Carlson, Carl Eloy, MM3c(T), USN
Kent, Wash.

Casey, Jack S., TM3c, USN
St. Louis, Mo.

Cassina, John (n), CTM, USN
Anacortes, Wash.

Cazale, John J., S1c, USN
Plymouth, Mass.

Chambers, William A., CM1c, USN
St. Augustine, Fla.

Champagne, Leodore, J., S1c, USNR
Wolfeboro, N. H.

Charlton, Nelson S., S1c, USNR
Warwick, R. I.

Choate, Laban D., CTM, USN
Terrell, Tex.

Choiniere, Joseph A., WT3c, USNR
Springfield, Mass.

Christensen, Edward M., Y3c(T),
USNR
Perth Amboy, N. J.

Christie, Henry T., S2c, USN
Brooklyn, N. Y.

Chrysler, John R., WT3c, USNR
Rodman, N. Y.

Churchill, Edward F., Jr., BM1c,
USN
Medford, Mass.

Cianca, Louis F., S1c, USN
Brooklyn, N. Y.

Cinq-Mars, Leo J., SF3c, USNR
Pawtucket, R. I.

Ciresi, Lawrence J., S1c, USNR
Brooklyn, N. Y.

Cislo, John A., S1c, USNR
Penns Grove, N. J.

Clay, Marvin Dale, SoM2c, USN
Mount Vernon, Wash.

Cmiel, Stanley (n), SC3c, USNR
Plymouth, Pa.

Conklin, Clarence R., WT2c, USN
Rockford, Ill.

Conklin, James A., RM2c, USN
Milwaukie, Ore.

Conklin, Robert S., WT2c, USN,
Rockford, Ill.

Conn, Charles R., Ensign, USNR
El Paso, Tex.

Conner, Joseph H., MM3c, USNR
Independence, Ia.

Conway, Clifford W., MoMM2c,
USNR
New York, N. Y.

Cook, James M., MM1c, USN
Ozark, Mo.

Crandell, Charles E., MM1c, USN
Westminster, Md.

Crider, Joe, M., WT3c, USNR
Kennett, Mo.

Cronberg, Donald B., WT1c(T),
USN
Minneapolis, Minn.

Crowley, Joseph P., Jr., EM1c,
USNR
Atlanta, Ga.

Custer, Lewis T., Cox, USN
Cambridge, Ind.

Cutler, John J., Jr., RM3c, USN
Berwyn, Ill.

Damstrom, Darven A., WT2c, USNR
Emmetsburg, Ia.

Daniel, Herschel C., GM2c, USNR
Jessup, Ga.

Daniels, Harold O., FC2c, USN
Humble, Tex.

Davidson, Willard C., CFC(AA)
USN
Aberdeen, S. D.

De Geeter, Morris A., EM2c, USNR
Moline, Ill.

Dendtler, Einar B., MM3c, USNR
Chicago, Ill.

Denney, Jasper J., Jr., S1c, USN
Olympia, Wash.

De Vegter, Floyd C., BM2c, USN
Brownsville, Tex.

Dirksen, Albert "T", SoM3c, USNR
Pembine, Wisc.

Disegni, Joseph M., WT3c, USN
New York, N. Y.

Dispoto, Charles, Jr., CM3c, USN
Hasbrouck Heights, N. J.

Dockendorff, Ernest W., Y1c, USNR
Randolph, Mass.

Donati, Herman T., Y2c, USNR
Dover, N. J.

Dorton, Jack C., BM2c, USN
Kingsport, Tenn.

Drobienski, Stanley, CMM, USN
Syracuse, N. Y.

Du Bois, Richard H., SK1c, USNR
Long Beach, Calif.

Duerr, Alfred, SF2c, USN
Valley Stream, L. I., N. Y.

Duke, Eugene P., M2c, USN
Goldsboro, N. C.

Duncan, Roy W., S1c, USNR
Sacramento, Calif.

Eborn, James M., Mo.MM2c, USNR
Washington, N. C.

Edwards, Archie R., CTM, USN
Chicago, Ill.

Esposito, Irvin, L., Cox, USN
Brooklyn, N. Y.

Evans, Darron H., FC1c, USN
Los Angeles, Calif.

Everett, George M., S1c, USN
Sylvatus, Va.

Fafara, Louis L., TM2c, USNR
Garfield, N. J.

Fama, Samuel C., SF2c, USNR
Glassboro, N. J.

Faulkner, Robert L., SM3c, USN
Montgomery, Ala.

Ferguson, Basil J., CEM, USN
Portland, Me.

Field, Robert F., MoMM2c, USNR
Okemos, Mich.

Finley, John M., Jr., WT2c, USN
Columbia, S. C.

Finnel, Patrick E., PhM1c, USNR
Browning, Mo.

Fleming, Robert H., WT2c, USN
Norfolk, Va.

Ford, Arthur G., WT3c, USNR
Detroit, Mich.

Foss, Ernest L., SC2c, USN
Springvale, Me.

Frekowicz, Joseph, S1c, USNR
Fall River, Mass.

Fronczak, Alfred M., Cox, USNR
North Tonowanda, N. Y.

Fuentes, Domingo, Jr., S1c, USNR
Elizabeth, N. J.

Gacka, Bernard, SK3c, USNR
Johnstown, Pa.

Gallaher, Murray E., CM, USNR
Vinton, Ia.

Gallinger, Morris T., SF2c, USN
Los Angeles, Calif.

Garland, Wilford W., F1c, USN
Bedford, Ind.

Garrison, William H., S1c, USN
Prue, Okla.

Gersch, Henry M., S1c, USN
Maspeth, N. Y.

Giannini, James W., MM2c, USNR
Conshohocken, Pa.

Giaquinto, Ralph J., MM2c, USNR
Brooklyn, N. Y.

Giroux, Terrence E., RdM3c,
Haverhill, Mass.

Glover, Sam O., CMoMM, USN
DeLeon, Tex.

Goetz, Donald G., Cox, USN
Los Angeles, Calif.

Goff, Frank R., SoM2c, USNR
Muskogee, Okla.

Goman, Edward T., S1c, USNR
Wilkes-Barre, Pa.

Goodrich, Lewis M., CY, USNR
Shamrock, Tex.

Gordon, Joseph W., Cox, USN
Brooklyn, N. Y.

Gordon, Robert W., SC1c, USNR
Wakefield, Mass.

Gotschall, Jack F., QM2c, USNR
Oakland, Calif.

Grasso, Daniel M., Y3c, USNR
Lodi, N. J.

Graver, Herbert H., SM3c, USNR
Mt. Pocono, Pa.

Gray, Millage, BM2c, USNR
Fairfax, Ala.

Gray, William F., S2c, USN
Atlanta, Ga.

Gregory, George E., B3c, USN
Bronx, N. Y.

Gregory, Ralph F., RM3c, USNR
Groves, Tex.

Gresavic, Joseph J., WT3c, USNR
Jackson Heights, N. Y.

Grove, Cyril A., EM3c, USNR
Scalp Level, Pa.

Guastella, Dominic J., FC3c, USNR
Brooklyn, N. Y.

Guess, George A., Jr., CRT(PA),
USN
Louisville, Ky.

Gynther, Eugene O., MM1c, USNR
Westerly, R. I.

Hadley, Donald L., MM2c, USNR
LaGrange, Ill.

Hagy, Charles H., Jr., MM1c, USNR
Baltimore, Md.

Hahn, Owen D., FCO1c(T), USNR
Swenson, Tex.

Hall, Richard J., Jr., FC3c, USNR
Union, N. J.

Halpin, Howard J., Cox, USNR
Elmont, N. Y.

Halter, Dale E., EM1c, USNR
Dover, O.

Hamilton, Claude L., Jr., Y1c, USN
Ingleside, Tex.

Hanke, George L., SK1c, USN
Norfolk, Va.

Hanna, Vern N., GM2c, USN
Colfax, Ia.

Harden, Charles R., EM1c, USNR
Ft. Lauderdale, Fla.

Hardin, Ambrose W., S1c, USNR
Dallas, N. C.

Harding, Warren B., Cox (T), USN
Washington, D. C.

Harper, Allen J., PhM2c, USN
Kinston, N. C.

Harris, Harry L., S1c, USN
Whiteville, N. C.

Hartman, Clayton E., Cox (T), USN
Philadelphia, Pa.

Hassay, Albert (n), F1c, USN
Youngstown, O.

Hayes, Thomas A., Bkr 3c, USNR
Sunfish, Ky.

Hays, Richard J., Jr., WT3c, USNR
Chicago, Ill.

Hefner, David J., EM2c, USNR
Dallas, Tex.

Herod, Nelson (n), S1c, USN
Burkeville, Tex.

Herr, Ernest A., CRM(AA), USNR
Bellevue, Pa.

Hibbitt, Raymond Ervin, BM1c,
USN
Burleson, Tex.

Hiemstra, Harold P., GM2c, USN
Dowagiac, Mich.

Hiller, Harry S., RM2c, USN
Williamsport, Pa.

Hockman, Dick S., GM3c, USNR
Mingoville, Pa.

Hofman, Philip R., WT3c, USN
Milwaukee, Wisc.

Holstius, John M., Cox, USN
New Bedford, Mass.

Honaker, Robert H., RM1c, USN
Lebanon, Va.

House, Herbert H., F1c, USNR
New Bern, N. C.

Howell, James "N", MM1c, USN
Benton Harbor, Mich.

Hoy, Howard W., B2c, USNR
Seattle, Wash.

Hreha, George J., RdM3c, USNR
Edinboro, Pa.

Hudgens, Clifford (n), GM3c, USN
DeRossett, Tenn.

Hudson, Joseph D., SM2c, USN
East Williston, N. Y.

Huggins, Mack (n), Chief Pay Clk.,
USN
Norfolk, Va.

Hull, John V., S1c, USNR
Rome, N. Y.

Hunt, Raymond V., MM2c, USNR
Arlington, Calif.

Huntley, Allen E., TM1c, USN
Findlay, O.

Husson, Alexander R., CSM(AA),
USN
Lynn, Mass.

Hutto, Charles S., M3c, USN
Augusta, Ga.

Isaacs, Paul G., RM2c, USN
Johnson City, Tenn.

Itzin, Lewis E., CWT(AA), USN
San Diego, Calif.

James, Frank C., MM2c, USNR
Cicero, Ill.

Janicki, Chester M., FC3c, USNR
Utica, N. Y.

Jefferson, Solomon J., StM1c, USN
New Orleans, La.

Jenkins, Weldon T., S1c, USNR
Compton, Calif.

Jessup, Max H., PhM1c, USN
Creston, Ia.

Johnson, Everett B., GM2c, USN
East Douglas, Mass.

Johnson, George W., RM1c, USN
Elizabethton, Tenn.

Johnson, Griffin D., Jr., St3c, USNR
Lewisburg, W. Va.

Johnson, Oren C., Jr., WT1c, USN
Wilmington, N. C.

Johnson, Seaborn L., EM3c, USN
Eugene, Ore.

Johnson, Valentine R., Jr., S1c, USNR
Newark, N. J.

Joiner, James H., CEM, USN
Florence Villa, Fla.

Jones, Edwin J., St3c, USN
Dallas, Tex.

Joseffy, William C., SM3c, USN
Maspeth, L. I., N. Y.

Kalinowski, Anthony S., CM2c, USNR
Gardner, Mass.

Keefe, Arthur W., Cox, USNR
Lowell, Mass.

Kenney, Francis A., GM2c, USNR
Oak Park, Ill.

Keppler, Edwell C., WT2c, USN
Coronado, Calif.

Kiewra, Edward J., S1c, USNR
Brooklyn, N. Y.

Kingsmore, Willis F., RM2c, USNR
Buffalo, S. C.

Kinsell, Finley G., MM3c, USNR
Lemont Furnace, Pa.

Kish, Joseph J., SoM2c, USNR
New Brunswick, N. J.

Kopsky, Stephen (n), MM1c, USN
Northport, N. Y.

Kosters, William H., GM3c, USNR
Hull, Ia.

Kotasek, Robert Y., GM1c, USN
Lakewood, O.

Koza, Elmer J., BM1c, USN
Akron, O.

Krieger, Elmer H. J., MM1c, USNR
Waterloo, Ia.

Kuehne, Carl A., GM1c, USN
Huntington Station, L. I., N. Y.

La Falce, Francis J., Cox., USNR
Newark, N. J.

Lanham, Richard N., CQM, USN
Baltimore, Md.

Lank, Merrill E., S1c, USNR
Eastport, Me.

Lapp, Arthur L., BM2c, USN
Macon, Mo.

Larsen, Walter H., SC1c, USNR
Bridgeport, Conn.

Lawrence, Edwin B., S1c, USNR
Lynn Grove, Ky.

Lewis, Olander K., StM2c, USN
Algiers, La.

Limacher, James F., MM1c, USNR
Milwaukee, Wisc.

Linden, Leroy J., WT2c, USNR
Pittsburgh, Pa.

Lindner, George R., F1c, USNR
Williamsville, N. Y.

Lloyd, Edward A., CMM, USN
Charleston, S. C.

Lord, Byron, BM2c, USNR
San Luis Obispo, Calif.

Lowder, Theodore A., S1c, USNR
Indianapolis, Ind.

Lowrance, James M., Bkr1c, USN
Kenton, Tenn.

Mabry, Horace R., MM1c, USN
Everett, Mass.

Mahool, Thomas, Jr., QM2c, USNR
Baltimore, Md.

Mallow, Henry M., CMM, USN
Peru, Ind.

Manley, Walter M., StM1c, USNR
Hurtsboro, Ala.

Marshall, Eugene J., CRN, USN
Independence, Mo.

Marshall, Jacob L., StM1c, USN
Wilmington, N. C.

Martin, Ernest S., Cox, USN
Long Beach, Calif.

Martin, James H., SC3c, USNR
Yampa, Colo.

Massey, Joe, S1c, USNR
Scurry, Tex.

Mattina, Vincenzo J., AS, USN
Boston, Mass.

McCook, James C., CPhM, USNR
Maynard, Mass.

McCown, Acker J., Jr., S1c, USN
Fort Worth, Tex.

McCue, Cornelius, WT3c, USNR
Springfield, Ill.

MacDonald, John P., GM3c, USN
Brooklyn, N. Y.

McFarling, William A., Jr., SKD2c,
  USNR
San Antonio, Tex.

McKee, Hiram J., RM1c, USN
Ponca City, Okla.

McMillan, Jay T., CSK, USN
Long Beach, Calif.

McWaters, William J., Cox, USN
McAlester, Okla.

Meier, Walter R., RdM3c, USNR
Shattuck, Okla.

Meyer, Harold R., S1c, USN
Minneapolis, Minn.

Meyer, Vernon L., GM1c, USNR
Dubuque, Ia.

Michalak, Tony V., S1c, USNR
Torrance, Calif.

Miller, Tellis T., GM1c, USN
Hickory, N. C.

Monahan, Robert F., TM3c, USNR
Dracut, Mass.

Moniz, Manuel, S1c, USNR
Fall River, Mass.

Moreau, Desire W., WT2c, USN
Duquesne, Pa.

Morse, Roland S., Jr., MoMM2c,
  USNR
Eliot, Me.

Mullins, Patrick J., S1c, USN
Hasbrouck Heights, N. J.

Murray, Glenn R., TM3c, USN
Dallas, Tex.

Muscott, Arthur R., TM1c, USNR
Battle Creek, Mich.

Nay, Clinton, CWT, USN
Antimony, Utah.

Neal, Jack D., AMM2c, USN
Detroit, Mich.

Nelson, Kenneth L., TMV3c, USN
Keokuk, Iowa.

Newborn, Eriah, CK1c, USN
Long Island City, N. Y.

Newton, W. L., SM2c, USNR
Brawley, Calif.

Nichum, Harold H., CM2c, USN
Los Angeles, Calif.

Norgan, Leslie H., Cox, USN
Sebeka, Minn.

Novinger, Francis L., Bkr 1c, USNR
Burlington, Kan.

O'Connor, Earl H., CPhM, USN
Berwick, Me.

Oliver, Joseph H., S1c(SM), USNR
Dadeville, Ala.

Olshark, Thomas A., S1c, USNR
Wilkes-Barre, Pa.

Ottiger, Otto M., GM1c, USN
Red Bud, Ill.

Padgett, Everett H., CRM, USN
Washington, D. C.

Papp, Alex F., GM3c, USNR
Trenton, N. J.

Pasciuti, Albert J., Cox, USNR
Framingham, Mass.

Peer, William H., MM1c, USNR
Cooper, Ia.

Peiffer, William R. EM1c, USNR
St. Louis, Mo.

Percy, Allen R., S1c, USN
Rodney, Mich.

Peterson, Carl P., TM1c, USN
St. Paul, Minn.

Peterson, George H., SC1c, USNR
Duluth, Minn.

Peterson, Harry C., S1c, USNR
Rockaway, N. J.

Peterson, Rudolf G., TM1c, USN
St. Paul, Minn.

Phee, William E., S1c, USN
Calais, Maine

Phelps, Hugh E., S1c, USNR
Albany, Ga.

Picton, Charles, CBM, USN
Annapolis, Md.

Pittman, Alvin E., F2c, USN
South Gate, Calif.

Pitts, Melvin E., S1c, USN
Sumiton, Ala.

Polak, Joseph S., CY(AA), USN
San Diego, Calif.

Popino, Kenneth E., B1c, USN
Firestone, Colo.

Poterjoy, Henry F., MM1c, USN
Ely, Minn.

Potthoff, George E., Jr., TM3c, USNR
Houston, Tex.

Potzer, Fred, Cox, USNR
Plymouth, Pa.

Rea, Gerald E., SoM2c, USN
Los Angeles, Calif.

Reid, Fred N., S1c, USNR
Burlington, Wyo.

Reith, Paul R., EM3c, USN
Alameda, Calif.

Rex, James W., SC2c, USNR
Springfield, Mass.

Rhyne, Will B., Mm1c, USNR
Charlotte, N. C.

Rial, Loren J., WT1c, USN
Fort Dodge, Ia.

Riley, Thomas A., SF3c, USN
Philadelphia, Pa.

Rios, Ruben H., F1c, USN
Kansas City, Mo.

Rivers, Rudolph W., Ck3c, USN
Charleston, S. C.

Roff, Raymond E., SC3c, USNR
Mt. Vernon, N. Y.

Rowland, Melvin E., MM3c(SR) USNR
Hydro, Okla.

Royer, Armand, S1c, USN
Montreal, Canada.

Ruffin, Rupert C., S1c, USN
Sherman, Tex.

Rumbo, Veloris R., F1c, USN
Monroe City, Mo.

Safford, Melvin L., MM1c, USNR
Watertown, N. Y.

Salamida, Joseph, SM2c, USNR
Albany, N. Y.

Sayen, Frank Emerson, S2c, USN
Pensacola, Fla.

Scarrozzo, James A., S1c, USNR
New Britain, Conn.

Schuchman, Philip M., B1c, USN
Foley, Mo.

Schultz, LaVerne M., S1c, USN
Whitehall, Wisc.

Schurk, Frederick J., SM2c, USNR
Fairfield, Conn.

Schymos, Howard L., CWT, USN
St. Louis, Mo.

Scott, Paul J., MM2c, USNR
Tacoma, Wash.

Scroggins, Olsen "F", S1c, USNR
Clayton, Ala.

Settlemyer, Carl H., CCM(PA), USN
Four Oaks, N. C.

Severs, Louis Michael, S2c, USN
Pittsburgh, Pa.

Sexton, Harold J., Cox, USN
Whittier, Calif.

Sexton, John Thomas, Lieutenant, USN
Stratford, Conn.

Shaparnis, Stanley (n), Cox, USN
Cleveland, O.

Shaw, John P., CWT(AA), USN
Salem, Mass.

Sheridan, John J., Y2c, USNR
Goshen, Ind.

Sheriff, John W., SM1c, USN
San Francisco, Calif.

Shirley, James L., RDM3c, USNR
Compton, Calif.

Smith, John W., S1c, USN
Schenectady, N. Y.

Smith, Lawrence J., EM2c, USNR
Newton, Mass.

Smith, Leland C., QM1c, USN
Merced, Calif.

Smith, Preston C., EM2c, USNR
Port Arthur, Tex.

Smith, William H., CMM, USN
Long Beach, Calif.

Smunk, Charles B., RM2c, USN
Goodwin, S. D.

Sousa, Frank J., Jr., RDM2c, USNR
Bristol, R. I.

Spencer, Oscar M., MM2c, USN
Spartanburg, S. C.

Spracklin, LeRoy H., BM1c, USN
New York, N. Y.

Starkey, George A., EM3c, USNR
Oklahoma City, Okla.

Starr, William C., GM3c, USNR
West Hartford, Conn.

Steil, William, SF1c, USNR
New York, N. Y.

Stevens, Charles E., S1c, USN
Powhatan Point, O.

Stinebiser, Henry Bernard, CMM
(PA), USN
San Rafael, Calif.

Swogger, Ralph E., S1c, USNR
Aliquippa, Pa.

Taylor, Otis, A., Jr., FCO3c(T),
USNR
Milwaukie, Ore.

Taylor, Thomas V., Jr., GM3c(T),
USNR
Pulaski, Tenn.

Ten Eyck, Hubert A., CGM(AA),
USNR
Tampa, Fla.

Teologo, Perfecto, Chief Steward,
USN
San Rogue, P. I.

Thompson, Howard F., TMV1c(T),
USNR
Lansing, Mich.

Tremble, Herman D., StM3c, USN
Kansas City, Mo.

Trenary, Floyd S., SC1c, USNR
Trenary, Mich.

Trevarton, George A., Sm3c, USNR
Long Mont, Colo.

Tronson, Robert Carl, CEM(PA),
USN
Highland, Calif.

Troxler, Leonard M., S1c, USNR
Hahnville, La.

Tuck, Jesse W., S1c, USN
Los Angeles, Calif.

Turner, John H., Ensign D-V(G),
USNR
Nashville, Tenn.

Uhrich, Fred L., MM1c, USN
Amarillo, Tex.

Unroe, Judson (n), Warrant Machinist, USN
Lesage, W. Va.

Ursini, Emil (n), CMoMM(AA),
USN
Cleveland, O.

Vails, Billy J., AS, USN
Seminole, Okla.

Valastro, Mario, S1c, USN
Lynn, Mass.

Vanderzander, Paul P., WT3c, USNR
Banks, Ore.

Vilbert, Jack, S2c, USNR
St. Louis, Mo.

Vorsino, John M., VM2c, USN
Grapeville, Pa.

Walker, David D., S1c, USNR
Renton, Wash.

Walsh, John P., Jr., SK2c, USN
Chicago, Ill.

Wasarhaley, William J., Jr., CEM,
USN
Berkeley, Calif.

Watson, Harold C., S1c, USN
Stockbridge, Mich.

Weeden, Melwart C., WT2c, USN
Richland Center, Wisc.

Whipple, Walter E., GM2c, USN
Oakland, Calif.

Whisler, Robert, S1c, USNR
Midland, Mich.

Whiteside, Burley, Ck3c, USN
Adamsville, Ala.

Wilkinson, Glenn E., Fc1c, USN
Valley Falls, R. I.

Wilson, Loren D., CMoM, USN
San Diego, Calif.

Winkley, Bruce E., GM2c, USNR
Eagle, Idaho.

Wood, James A., CMM, USNR
New York, N. Y.

Wood, Louis E., EM3c, USNR
Broken Arrow, Okla.

Wrenn, Edwin T., CBM, USN
Hodges, S. C.

Wright, Robert L., CMM, USN
Long Beach, Calif.

Wrisley, Ernest V., CMM, USNR
Elizabethtown, N. Y.

Yurecko, Michael, Jr., GM2c, USN
Hillside, N. J.

Zanghi, Angelo A., Cox, USNR
Brocton, N. Y.

Zarnecki, Frank J., RM3c, USNR
Erie, Pa.

Zeigler, Marland J., QM2c, USN
New Oxford, Pa.

Zimmerman, Mack M., CWT, USN
Etowah, Tenn.